Suicide Weapon

Suicide Weapon

A J Barker

Editor-in-Chief: Barrie Pitt
Editor: David Mason
Art Director: Sarah Kingham
Picture Editor: Robert Hunt
Designer: David A Evans
Cover: Denis Piper
Special Drawings: John Batchelor
Photographic Research: John Moore
Cartographer: Richard Natkiel

First Printing: June 1971
Printed in United States of America

Ballantine Books Inc.
101 Fifth Avenue New York NY 10003

An Intext Publisher

Contents

Futile sacrifice

Introduction by Barrie Pitt

A mere handful of words from Japanese has been absorbed into English. They naturally include a number of place and personal names, but also there are terms from Japanese buddhism: Zen, satori, koan; the arts: haiku, netsuki, bonsai, origami, kabuki and No; food: sukiyaki, sake; dress: kimono; finance: yen; social position: geisha, samurai, mikado; transport: the bastard 'rickshaw'; sport: jui-jitsu, dan, karate; natural phenomena: tsunami; and so on. But more powerfully emotive than these, and symbolizing for the West those aspects of the Japanese make-up at once so fearful and so fascinating, are the words harakiri, banzai – and kamikaze.

In English 'kamikaze' has come to be applied more broadly than its original meaning; hence the title of this book, which deals with all the manifestations of the Japanese fighting man's readiness – indeed, eagerness – to volunteer unthinkingly for certain death. In its first use in the Second World War it was the official designation of those groups of fighter pilots who were invited, and willingly agreed, to set out on missions whose specific aim was to crash their bomb carrying aircraft into Allied ships as the only way of restoring the lost parity in offensive strength. The initial success of these missions stimulated a mounting effort to produce purpose-built manned torpedoes and rocket and jet powered winged bombs in which the pilot's function was nothing more nor less than to provide reliable guidance up to the moment of impact; his function

was completed at the moment of the explosion which inevitably destroyed him.

There have always been, as A J Barker points out, cases in war where exceptionally brave and determined men have deliberately chosen to perform heroic deeds certain to result in their deaths. Usually this is because they know their situation to be hopeless in any event, or in order to shield a comrade, or because of the extreme emotional involvement of the moment. But the planned and systematized suicide tactics of the Japanese in the latter part of the Second World War were something else again.

To begin to understand the frame of mind of a nation whose every member seemed to the Allies willing to die by its own hand rather than acknowledge defeat, it will be worth glancing at some aspects of her history. Geographically Japan bears a relationship to eastern Asia similar to the relationship of the British Isles to continental Europe. However, the Straits of Dover are only some twenty-three miles wide, and at its closest – opposite Korea – Japan is distant from the mainland more than four times this figure. A very significant difference for the passage of goods, ideas and armies in the days of sailing ships.

The near-by stimulus of the constantly intriguing and warring European kingdoms kept England evolving socially and materially in a way denied to Japan, separated as she was from the monolithic – and itself conservative – Chinese Empire by the wastes of the China Sea. Thus Japan remained essentially mediaeval throughout the centuries during which the European states were undergoing their successive renaissances, ages of learning and industrial revolutions; and additionally, due partly to unfortunate experiences, foreign commerce and influence were excluded as a matter of deliberate policy.

When at last, in the late 1860s, Japan opened her doors to western ideas and started on her meteoric and highly successful career of industrialization, she was still in all major respects a feudal society. The ruling samurai class, becoming the new nation's educators as well as its administrators and military chiefs, were at pains to keep it so. The habit of unquestioning subservience to and even worship of authority was stringently maintained, surviving intact the wave of cultural and political iconoclasm which inevitably accompanied the influx of new ideas and techniques. One still obeyed the God-Emperor (and, by a kind of papal extension, his appointees), as one always had; not because being Emperor he was in a position to enforce obedience, or because he was qualified to rule, or from affection, or even from what a western man would understand by loyalty, but simply and finally because he was The Emperor. And the preservation of 'face' remained an overriding consideration in all activities.

On this favourable foundation the armed forces built, reinforcing ingrained social attitudes with what amounted to brainwashing; and adding the conceit, particularly pleasing to an emergent nation, that the Japanese were an inherently superior race, destined to rule.

In 1895, less than thirty years after breaking her policy of isolation, Japan defeated China; a decade later, Russia. Soon she was competing successfully in world markets, originating where earlier she had copied. The self-confidence engendered by these undoubtedly enormous achievements became an arrogance which led her to make unreasonable demands on her neighbours, and ultimately, with Hitler's war under way, to challenge the United States of America with the attacks on Pearl Harbor and the Philippines and invade wherever her arm would reach in the Pacific and South-east Asia.

The first months of the war served only to strengthen her good opinion of herself as victory followed victory, but the reckoning was on the way. Inevitably the superior resources and industrial potential of the United States and her determination to wipe out the humiliation of Pearl Harbor resulted in the slow but sure outstripping of Japanese power in the Pacific. A series of reverses and the decisive defeat at Guadalcanal – despite the committal of every Japanese plane, ship and soldier that could be spared – demonstrated that the tide was on the turn. Since to every Japanese serviceman and civilian defeat was inconceivable, any and every imaginable method to achieve victory had to be employed. Thus it was that Vice-Admiral Ohnishi came to make the proposal that escalated into the kamikaze programme.

There followed the manifold horrors of the closing phase of the Pacific War. Hundreds of thousands of lives were uselessly thrown away for the reason that no other course of action was compatible with honour. To many of those in power the death of a nation was preferable to the loss of face involved in capitulation. It is entirely possible that had the atomic bombs not fallen on Hiroshima and Nagasaki it would have been necessary to mount a full scale invasion involving the loss of millions of lives.

The great 17th century poet Matsuo Basho wrote a *haiku* whose subject is the futility of war; he could well have been mourning the lost generation of Japanese soldiery which lies buried in the Pacific battlefields.

Summer grasses–
All that remains
Of soldiers' visions.

On 11th August 1945, peace-drunk crowds in London's Piccadilly, New York's Times Square, and scores of other Allied cities congregated to celebrate the news that Japan had tentatively accepted the Allied terms for surrender. The war in the Far East was over, and for three days the crowds made merry.

But the celebrations were premature. At the fronts men were still fighting and dying; in Tokyo only a handful of people knew that the surrender was even a possibility.

Prologue

Americans celebrate VJ-Day in Times Square, New York

render. Their aim was a *gyokusai* – an Armageddon – which would turn Japan back to the Stone Age from its once sophisticated industrial complexity. The more blood that was drawn the better the chances of the Allies settling for less in order to stop the slaughter. If need be the whole Japanese nation would commit suicide.

As so often before in Japan the centre of ferment was the army. Despite the appalling devastation of Hiroshima and Nagasaki many of the officers were bitterly opposed to surrender and occupation. A *coup* was planned, and there were sporadic outbursts in some parts of the country, but this particular *putsch* fizzled out. Meanwhile on the evening of 13th August there was a meeting of the chiefs of the Operations Sections of the Army and Navy General Staffs and the chief of the Military Affairs Section of the War Ministry to discuss the Government's proposal to accept the surrender terms. Admiral Takajiro Ohnishi, the developer and high priest of the Kamikaze corps, was the principal naval representative and by the end of the meeting he was in tears. 'We must submit to the Emperor a plan to gain victory . . . If we are resolute and are prepared to sacrifice twenty million Japanese lives in a Kamikaze effort victory will be ours!'

Fortunately the pleas of the suicide specialist were not taken seriously by the rest of the meeting. Ohnishi was not finished, for he then tried to persuade Prince Takamatsu, a younger brother of the Emperor who had served in the Imperial Navy, to influence the Emperor in favour of a decisive battle. Takamatsu would not even listen and when Ohnishi left him in the early hours of the morning of 14th August, he said to a staff officer 'All is over!'

In fact all was not over and there was still the possibility of a Japanese

Most believed that all Japanese must fight on, with *Yamato* spirit if not with modern weapons. Even many of those who knew the nation was on the brink of surrender refused to consider it. And there were others who not only rejected the idea of surrender but were determined to prevent it. Some of these men were even prepared to commit Japan to total destruction – to bring down the roof of Japanese civilisation in a Samsonesque finale – rather than submit to the indignity of unconditional sur-

Götterdämmerung. The army had grounded most of its planes and on the 14th the Chief of Staff ordered them all to be disarmed and their fuel tanks removed. The navy was not prepared to accept the nothingness that was about to descend on them quite so easily however. The 302nd Air Group at Atsugi airfield outside Tokyo – the training ground for kamikaze pilots – refused to accept defeat and the commandant, Captain Yasuna Kozono, led a group of diehards on a leaflet raid over Tokyo. The leaflets declared that it would be wrong to surrender and that it was not the Emperor who wanted to give up but 'traitors round the Throne.' There were 2,000 men at Atsugi who had completed kamikaze training, and they were filled with the mindless longing to go and die for the Emperor which their training had inculcated. Led by Kozono, they boasted they would torpedo the Allied fleet in Tokyo Bay and blow its flagship, the battleship *Missouri*, out of the water.

Kozono was a capable pilot, a brave man and a good commander, who had maintained a high standard of discipline in his group and kept his aircraft in fighting trim despite the deteriorating conditions in the rest of the country. He was also a fanatic, and when he was ordered to prepare Atsugi airfield to receive the vanguard of the occupation forces, he refused. Threats that force would be used to compel his obedience to orders were ignored, and he was deprived of his command only by a trick.

Another of the last-ditch diehards who refused to accept the idea of surrender was the famous Captain Minoru Genda, who had organised the air attack on Pearl Harbor. Genda was then commanding one of the few remaining groups of fighter planes in Japan. However, when he was finally assured that it was the Emperor's will to end the war Genda used his own

Vice-Admiral Takijiro Ohnishi, the advocate of crash-dive tactics

considerable prestige with the hotheads in the air force and persuaded them to accept the end quietly. Luckily for General MacArthur's troops, discipline held and a special message from the Emperor to the Japanese armed forces clinched matters. The Japanese people were not to embark on suicidal operations; there was to be no *Götterdämmerung*.

Nevertheless there were some who were prepared to resist to the bitter end. The fanatical Atsugi kamikaze pilots continued their revolt up to about the time when MacArthur arrived. And when the occupation troops did start to land more than a thousand Japanese army officers as well as hundreds of naval officers and civilians dispatched their spirits to the Yasukuni Shrine by taking their own lives. Many of them saw suicide as the only rational escape from a chaotic world in which their standards had suddenly vanished. Some of those who took this action did so to express guilt and protest – not as a final aggressive backlash against society as in the West. It was not a ritual act demanded of them by the Emperor, the government, or the military system. Unlike the classic Western case where the condemned officer is left alone with a bottle of brandy and a pistol, no overt pressure was put on these Japanese.

Yet many more responded to the defeat as others had done to the 1932 London naval treaty which had stirred such violent emotions in Japan. Then, as in 1945, they took their lives as an ultimate act of protest against a decision they could not change. At the war's end, others – in the spirit of earlier days – took on their shoulders the responsibility for the failure of their subordinates and ultimately themselves in their duty to the Emperor. A few who feared being arraigned as war criminals no doubt chose death before dishonour.

Some organised a dramatic scene for their self-destruction. Admiral Ohnishi, the father of the Kamikazes

Jubilant crowds in London's
Piccadilly Circus celebrate V-J Day

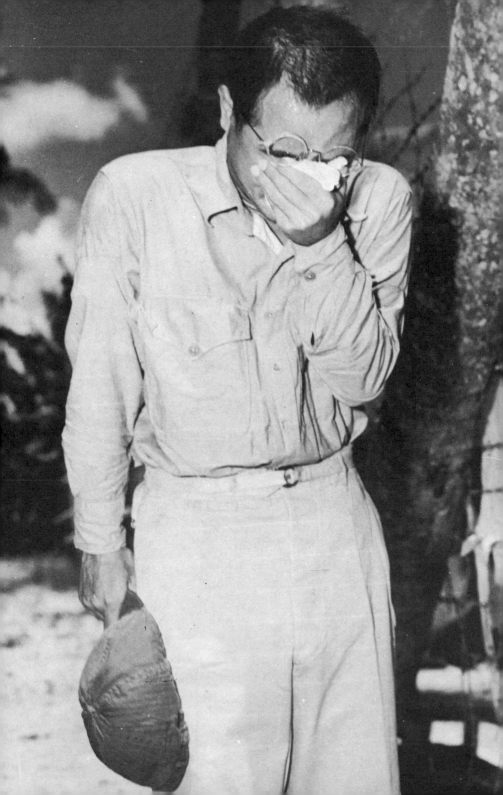

Left: A Japanese POW weeps on hearing the news of the Japanese surrender
Above left: Field-Marshal Sugiyama and (*above right*) General Tanaka; both committed suicide after the unconditional surrender

and advocate of a suicidal war ended his life in the early hours of 16th August. The event was carefully staged in his official residence and he disemboweled himself in the traditional manner. On his desk he left an emotional message saying that he apologized with his suicide to the souls of the men he had ordered to their doom and to their bereaved families.

In contrast to Ohnishi's exit one of his subordinates took a more conventional way out. On 14th August, Navy HQ in Tokyo ordered that all kamikaze operations should be suspended. However when the commanding officer of the 5th Air Fleet heard that Japan would surrender he decided that his duty lay in disobeying the command, and Vice-Admiral Matome Ugako chose one final suicide attack as his act of defiance. With ten other Kamikazes following, he took off from Oita airfield, and headed for Okinawa to attack enemy ships. None of them returned. It had been Ugako's duty to send kamikaze pilots against the enemy and he thought it appropriate to perish as had his men.

Marshal Sugiyama, a former war minister, carefully arranged his demise for the maximum symbolic effect. On the day his troops were demobilized the marshal shot himself, while his wife – by prearrangement – stabbed herself to death in front of the Shinto altar in their home. General Tanaka, who had been refused permission to commit *hari-kiri* at a Colour burning ceremony in front of his troops, shot himself through the head seated at his desk on which he had placed a statue of the Emperor Meiji, his will, a scroll given to him by Emperor Hirohito, his cap, sword, gloves . . . and false teeth.

Tanaka, Sugiyama and Ohnishi were among the men at the top who ended their lives because Imperial Japan did not fight on. They were but a handful of those who chose death; the soil of the imperial plaza in front of the Emperor's palace was drenched with the blood of suicides for days after the final surrender. They were Japan's final sanguine sacrifices in the Second World War – the last use of a terrible weapon which shocked the world.

'The Japanese who surrendered would never again be able to hold his head up in Japan'; some paid the price

Suicide
and bushido

In no society has suicide ever been so much of an institution as in the Japan which changed its face in 1945. Tokyo still records seven suicides per day and although this rate is no higher than in the enlightened United States of America the significant thing about suicide in Japan is the motivation and the ecstasy in which it is usually committed. Love-sick youngsters deciding their mutual attachment to be hopeless have been known to write notes committing their souls to union in the next incarnation, and then tie themselves together and jump into volcanic craters or hurl themselves into the path of an oncoming express train. Others, unable to arrange the romantic double act, would do so individually. And if the self-sacrifice were staged properly as like as not it would initiate a whole series of similar suicides. As an example, after the newspapers had played up the romantic death of a love-sick youth in the smoking crater of Mount Mihara on Hachijojima

Island, 149 people were known to have followed him into the crater within a year. 688 other would-be suicides were restrained by the police – the oldest being a man of sixty-five, the youngest a girl of fifteen. Family troubles and sickness accounted for many, but the only explanation for the majority, who were between twenty and thirty, was that they were suffering from a kind of suicide hysteria.

The type of Japanese hysteria with which the Western World was concerned between 1941 and 1945 was that which was tied up with national pride and the Emperor Hirohito. As a protest against Japan's surrender to America and Great Britain at the London naval conference in 1930, Lieutenant Kusukara committed *harikiri* with his officer's sword, kneeling in his night clothes in a narrow-gauged train berth. That was really the beginning of the agitation which brought about the downfall of the government, the seizure of Manchuria, the withdrawal of Japan from the League of Nations, and preparations for a war with the United States, Britain and Russia if need be. When Admiral Takarabe, chief naval delegate to the London conference, arrived home, he was met, of course, by a patriot who elaborately presented to him a dagger with which to commit suicide. Later a twenty-six-year-old student of political science appeared at the admiral's office, read a high-powered protest, and slit open his own belly in the presence of the admiral's secretary.

In due course the assassinations of premiers, plutocrats, and liberals took place. This emotional frenzy reached its climax at the civil, military and naval trials of the young patriot-assassins in the fall of 1933. It was no flash in the pan. Guided by a certain junior army officer, Hideki Tojo (who in 1942 was to become the warlord of the west Pacific, and

19

Premier of Japan),it was rooted deep in the emotional life of the Japanese people, bolstered by historical incidents, and supported by most of the Japanese newspapers and millions of soldiers, sailors, officers, and the populace. Less spectacular outbursts of emotion prevalent at this time were also significant. A man named Nojima, sending the minister of the Interior a five-foot long petition for unemployment relief accompanied it with his finger. Three non-commissioned officers at Shanghai tied dynamite on their backs, went into the Chinese barbed-wire defences, and set themselves off. They are now enshrined in the great military museum in Tokyo. Their mothers were taken about the islands on a special train and tens of thousands pressed forward to kiss the hems of their kimonos. Japanese in Peru sent money for the erection of a monument to the *san yushi* (three heroes). Mrs Chiyo (Willow) Inouye, learning that her doctor husband was to go with the medical corps to Manchuria, put on her wedding kimono and cut her throat, leaving the following letter:

'To my dear husband: My heart is filled to the brim with gladness. I cannot find words to congratulate you. Before you depart for the front tomorrow, I leave this world to-day.

'Please do not worry about your home, for there is no longer anything to make you worry. Powerless as I am, I am doing what little I can so that you and your men may fight with heart and soul for the country. That is all I wish and no more.

'Thanks to your kindness, my life has been happy. Though this world is ephemeral, the next world, it is said, is eternal. Some day you will come to join me there. I shall be waiting for you.

'They say it is very cold in Manchuria. Please take care to keep warm.

'I enclose herewith forty yen. When

**'Our highest hope is to die for him';
Emperor Hirohito**

you reach the front, please distribute it among the soldiers.

'I pray for your success.

Your wife.'

Such was the mediaeval emotionalism which lay behind the totalitarian state determined in 1940 to secure its place in the sun. Its people had been indoctrinated with theories of their superiority and their divine mission to liberate the East from Western domination. Its military commanders had long foreseen that a war in Europe would give them a free hand in Asia and when it came they were ready. For years the nation had been on a war footing and all the necessary preparations had been completed for a war with both the United States and Britain. Two and a half million men under arms waited the Emperor's call to sweep through Asia and across the Pacific to free its subject peoples; from the radio stations propaganda emphasizing the divine mission was poured out. The generals and admirals pointed at Australia and India; some even spoke of victory parades in London and Washington.

Their soldiers, sailors and aviators accepted the predictions for the future with equanimity born of oriental fatalism. Contemporary Japanese poets had compared these 'warriors' with the cherry blossom cultivated in Japan for its flower, and which the Japanese people regard as a symbol of purity, loyalty and patriotism, but whose beauty is shortlived. The life of the Japanese soldier was said to be like that of the cherry blossom.

'The cherry is first among blossoms, The warrior is first among men.'

His life was dedicated to his country: when the time came it should be laid down without hesitation. In his elementary school he had been taught to love his nation with a passion that no Westerner knows. The Japanese soldier served his Emperor with pride, and accepted an iron discipline and the influence of the Samurai spirit without question. 'Do or die; death before dishonour': this was his code, and the basis of Bushido. And the nation believed in, and had the deepest respect for, its army. If the generals said that they would conquer the world, then doubtless they would, or their armies would perish in the attempt.

It was the soldier to whom Japan owed her successes; he has been contemptuously described as an 'ant', a 'beaver', or an 'insect', but it was of him that Field-Marshal Slim, the distinguished commander of Britain's Fourteenth Army in Burma, said: 'We talk a lot about fighting to the last man and the last round, but the Japanese soldier is the only one who actually does it.'

It was never even necessary to order a Japanese soldier to hold on to the last man and the last round, he had, in fact, to be ordered to forget his honourable intentions and withdraw. To show his back to the enemy was cowardly and to do so brought dishonour on the soldier's family name; the greatest honour that he could hope to achieve was to die for the Emperor. On this basis the Japanese High Command assumed that all soldiers were equally brave and consequently there was no medal for valour like the Victoria Cross or the Congressional Medal of Honour. Medals were only given for campaigns or long and distinguished service. Since the code of military conduct did not countenance surrender, it was ignominious. And because the Geneva Prisoner of War Convention ran counter to this point of view Japan never ratified it. An Allied soldier who fought to the last round finding himself facing hopeless odds suffered no disgrace if he surrendered. In similar conditions the only honourable course open to the Japanese soldier was to fight to the death, keeping the last round for himself if necessary. Alternatively he could charge the enemy in a final suicidal attack. Even if he were taken prisoner after being wounded and unable to move or unconscious, he would never again be able to hold his head up in Japan. In such circumstances he would often try to commit suicide. For those who surrendered to him his feelings were generally of utter contempt; such men in his eyes were dishonoured, and had forfeited any right to consideration.

Yet despite the behaviour of their soldiers, fatalistic resignation to death is not inherent in the Japanese character; there were just as many young men trying to avoid conscription as there were in Britain and the United States and the same subterfuges were used in attempts to gain exemption. Once they were in the army, however, it was not long before their attitude altered. Recruits were subjected to an intense three-month course of indoctrination which changed them into fanatics, ready to die for their emperor, their country and the honour of their regiment. Slapping, kickings and savage discipline hardened them. 'Pain and pity will make men of you', the sergeant-major would shout at recruits; 'When we've done with you, you'll be able to murder without shedding a tear.' The slogan 'Our highest hope is to die for the Emperor' was chanted until it became a positive obsession, and every evening the army would ceremoniously turn its face towards the invisible palace of the God-Emperor and recite the words of the Imperial Rescript . . . 'Death is lighter than a feather, but duty is higher than a mountain.' This served to remind the soldier of his sacred mission and of the glorious reward, *Senshi* – death in battle.

Nor was the indoctrination of the serviceman's family forgotten either; soon after the new recruit was called up, his relatives would receive a letter from his commanding officer asking them to be careful not to block his road to an honourable death. The effectiveness of the propaganda may

Two presidents of the National Women's League bow to departing troops

be judged from Mrs Inouye's suicidal letter. Many officers and men even had their funeral rites performed before leaving for the front to show their intention of dying for their country and one of the marching songs included the mournful lines:

' Whether I float as a corpse under the water, or sing beneath the grasses of the mountain-side, I will willingly die for the Emperor.'

With men trained in this outlook a call for volunteers for a forlorn hope invariably produced plenty ready to face certain death.

Most people consider staying alive to be more attractive and useful than being dead and even the Japanese recruit had to be convinced. So, in order to give the prospect of death more appeal certain benefits were promised. Army textbooks postulated that, 'To die for the sake of the Emperor is to live for ever', and it became standard practice for attacks to culminate in death-defying 'banzai' charges. So far as death was con-

'Those who surrendered had forfeited any right to consideration'. *Above and right:* Sikh prisoners are used for rifle and bayonet practice

cerned, 'No matter how much of a wrongdoer,' said a Tokyo newspaper, 'no matter how evil a Japanese subject may have been, when once he has taken his stand on the field of battle all his past sins are atoned for and they become as nothing. The wars of Japan are carried on in the name of the Emperor and are therefore holy wars. All the soldiers who participate in these holy wars are representatives of the Emperor . . . those who have consummated tragic death in battle, whether they are good or bad are sanctified.' In spite of all this propaganda something of the normal person's attitude still lingered; even if they did accept that they were going out to die most soldiers wore a *sennin-bari* – a cloth band containing stitches of hair from a thousand women which supposedly kept its wearer from harm – round their waists. Such faith was placed in this particular charm that female relatives would walk the streets and solicit passers-by for a strand of hair to bring protection to their loved ones. But, if luck failed and the soldier 'consummated tragic death in battle' he was deemed to have joined the Gods, and his soul was enshrined in the Yasukuni temple in Tokyo. 'See you in Yasukuni' was a catch phrase among Japanese soldiers, and when they parted before battle they meant it. In Yasukuni they would finish up in the care of the Japanese Kami, the gods of nationalism, and stand guard over the sacred islands of Japan; this they were led to believe was a cause for exultation.

Consideration for the role to be played amongst the gods after death normally resulted in the Japanese taking considerable trouble to recover their dead after a battle. The corpses would be cremated but if this was not possible they would try to burn a portion of the body – even fingernail parings were sufficient – to send back ashes to the bereaved family at home. Then, twice a year during the period of the war, an elaborate ceremony was staged at Yasukuni when the names of the war dead were placed in an ark which was carried in a torch-light procession up to the altar where the names were deified. Thereafter the soldier reputedly continued to fight for Japan in the spirit world.

'Bushido' soon gained the Japanese soldiers a reputation for implacable ferocity on every battlefield on which they fought. Men were driven to exhaustion point with complete disregard for normal human feelings and officers treated them with a barbaric severity. Whilst their conduct towards their prisoners was above reproach during the Russo-Japanese war, the story of the post-1930 era was very

Victorious Japanese troops on the walls of Nanking, China

different, and prisoners of war were treated with bestial harshness. Many Japanese troops regarded the prisoners as being lucky to be alive but the very fact they were necessitated lack of consideration; a similar attitude was displayed towards the majority of the Asian peoples of the occupied territories. Somewhat naturally this eventually dissipated any goodwill that the new citizens of the co-prosperity sphere might have had for their 'liberators'. This is not to say that the Government in Tokyo had no understanding of the problems of Asian nationalism, but civilian administrators sent to the occupied countries from Tokyo were subservient to the military commanders, by whom they were generally regarded as inferior.

Much of the respect for the ability of Japanese soldiers was well deserved. When everything was going according to plan they were superb fighters. In the early days of the war, whilst the British and Americans were still learning their tactics from painful experiences in Burma and the Philippines, great stress was laid on their cleverness and skill. Their apparent competence in staging night attacks, their trickery and fanatical courage all had the effect of developing a sense of inferiority in the British and US soldiers, particularly when these qualities were given dramatic press coverage. In practice the Japanese were not so adept as many of the press reports suggested. However they were not prepared to sit in defended localities and do nothing; their successes depended entirely on offensive operations. If they were quiet in one area of the front they were generally preparing a surprise on the flanks. And this fighting characteristic was more than a mere tactical doctrine: it was a deep-seated attitude of mind which would seek expression even in the most desperate situation. 'There are few of us left and we have no arms . . .' a soldier diarist wrote, ' but those of us who are left are to carry out a

night attack from about 4 o'clock.' The word 'defence' was avoided; Japanese staff officers preferred to say that a position 'would be secured for an advance.'

Snipers were employed to an extent that was unprecedented in any other army and their activities served to perpetuate the terrors of the battlefield long after a successful assault on a Japanese position, or after an attack had been repulsed. These men would remain concealed and motionless, waiting patiently for hours on end for a suitable target to present itself – preferably one who, by his badges or behaviour showed that he was an officer. Fortunately for many of the luckless targets the Japanese was often a comparatively poor shot, but he remained an unknown quantity who struck terror in the hearts of inexperienced troops. It was some time before the Allies developed anti-sniper tactics.

But it was not true that the Japanese soldier had 'thrown away the book' as was frequently said in the early days of the war. It was certainly true that he was able to slip through the jungle, particularly at night, but the qualifying expression 'silently and invisibly', so often quoted in the Press, was rarely true. Contary to popular belief, the Japanese had done little actual jungle training before their campaign in Malaya, and even in 1944 they were anything but silent. The presence of their patrols was frequently disclosed by constant chattering and conversations. It was their predilection for night attacks which was most disturbing to Allied troops. In the darkness they would attack along well-defined paths or follow white-cloth markers tied to bushes by earlier patrols which would help to maintain their sense of direction. The attacks would be preceded by a considerable amount of noise and shooting, followed by a mass rush with

Japanese forces gain a reputation for implacable ferocity

loud cries of 'Banzai'. Frequently there would also be taunts and misleading commands in English. Often the rush would be sufficient to swamp the defender's resistance and invariably they remained dangerous and fanatical in their courage, no matter what casualties they suffered in the attack. There was no lack of ingenuity, they were quick to pick up the names that they heard, and then call out to these individuals from the darkness. Similarly with passwords, until the British and US troops selected words which the Japanese had difficulty in pronouncing: words like 'velvet' of which their pronunciation sounded like 'berubet'.

One of the much-quoted advantages of the Japanese soldier was his ability to exist for a week on a bag of rice and a drink from the village pond, whilst his Allied counterparts, compelled to exist in a similar fashion, soon fell sick. It was also said that the Japanese were more capable of accepting physical hardships. In fact their stamina was no different. Japanese and Allied soldiers all got just as wet when it rained, and suffered just as much. Malaria, dysentery, typhus, and other forms of tropical disease affected both sides in the same way. The essential difference lay in the fact that the Allied sick were still regarded as valuable individuals who had to be cared for, whilst the Japanese rarely considered a man to be sick until he was at death's door. Even then such men would be regarded as contemptibly weak. The result of the Allied regard for their casualties was a drag on their communications; the Japanese had no such problem. The pay-off lay in the return of many of the Allied casualties to the battle, whilst many of the Japanese casualties literally starved to death.

The Japanese attitude to the jungle

Above left: Japanese troops ford a river; their successes depended upon offensive operations. *Left:* Officer training school cadets parade

31

Left: Japanese marines train in the 'bushido' tradition. *Above:* Hirohito's troops bow towards the Imperial Palace before a campaign starts. *Below:* Part of the elaborate burial ceremony for a Japanese soldier

Above: 'Pain and pity will make men of you': the slogan of the Japanese soldier. *Left:* Nanking falls as part of the early Japanese success

was wasted . . . even the section leaders could not be lined up . . . 1st class Pte Hirose was killed by an enemy bullet. Corporal Hamada was unable, due to darkness, to assemble the men remaining. . . because of the darkness two men and I took the wrong turning.'

Stress was laid on fighting rather than parade-ground qualities and their dress could only be described as sloppy although the officers often made up for the appearance of their troops by parading in coloured sashes. And with swords that seemed strangely out of place and too big for their squat bodies the officers sometimes presented a musical comedy appearance. They would drive their men unmercifully to a point which no Allied soldier would ever have accepted and which would seem sometimes to be beyond the limit of human endurance. All this the Japanese soldier would accept with unhesitating obedience. Squalor, lack of food and punishment were his service life. He could expect little in the way of amenities except perhaps an occasional visit to a Japanese 'comfort girls' establishment, and even his pleasures there were conditioned by his rank.

'Impregnable, unsinkable, invulnerable' were popular Tokyo epithets. The concept of the Imperial Japanese Army and Navy had been formulated around the word 'Attack' and placed too much confidence in fighting spirit. Once the Japanese were forced on to the defensive, they were lost. Their courage rarely failed; the failure lay in the intelligent use of this courage. And difficulties which they got themselves into by coming to believe their own propaganda and deceiving themselves may be imagined. There was 'dishonour' in reporting the loss of a battle. But there was no dishonour in losing men – that suggested bravery. In 1944, when the prospect of defeat loomed over Japan it seemed logical to combine suicide and bushido – dutiful death with honour – into an official military weapon.

was probably more realistic than that of the Allies. They had seen that certain features of the jungle offered advantages to the soldier which no other terrain did, and they had quickly adapted their equipment and tactics to utilize these advantages. This all contributed to their reputation of being the superhuman jungle soldiers that has already been discussed. But they had the same human failings as any other soldiers. They got lost in the dark or confused in a battle in just the same way. The diary of a Japanese platoon commander records problems that could well have been those of his enemy: 'As dusk approached we approached to within seventy metres of the enemy . . . because of our faulty formation and the hindering rain we were unable to carry out the charge . . . Decided to attack at night, but men were not properly assembled . . . valuable time

Banzai:
10,000 years
for the Emperor

east tip of the island, where an American battalion was left to hold it until what was left could be finished off. One night however, a large group of the Japanese broke out of the trap and headed for the airfield which the Americans had established on the island. Considering the circumstances the operation was unusually well organised and orders were issued that 'Those who cannot participate . . . must commit suicide'. 'Casualties will remain in the present position and defend the area' into which the detachment had been driven. The password was *Shichi Sei Hokuku* (Seven lives for one's country) – meaning evidently that each man was supposed to kill seven Americans before going to join his ancestors. In addition they were to do as much damage as possible to the installations and aircraft on the airstrip and try to get through to their own lines to the north.

Exactly how many started out on this fantastic sortie will never be known. Some 500 bodies were counted the following morning, and it is possible that a number of Japanese got through to the shelter of the jungle, if not to their own lines. In this case, the attack was singularly unsuccessful. Not only did they fail to kill 'seven for one', but when they got to the airfield they were driven off before they had had an opportunity to do much damage there. Three days later however, there was another Japanese offensive which was a much more serious business. 'The fight on Saipan as things now stand is progressing one-sidedly' the Japanese commander reported to Tokyo. 'Step by step he comes towards us and concentrates his fire on us as we withdraw . . .' This was the situation which General Saito was determined to break.

Saito, an old man, had recognized the writing on the wall for some time.

Harsh training developed the Japanese soldier's powers of endurance, and by the time he joined his regiment he was rarely troubled by any inhibiting battle ethics. He knew that his task was to win battles, by achieving surprise if possible; otherwise by overwhelming the enemy with sheer weight of numbers and indifference to loss. If need be he had to die in the process; death was his destiny. Officers and men alike were essentially attack minded. All Japanese manuals and field regulations emphasized the offensive aspect of warfare, and the curious phenomenon of the Banzai charge was the culmination of this philosophy of attack. Throughout the war, wherever the Japanese fought there were Banzai charges designed to show the superiority of the spiritual power 'behind Hirohito's devil-subduing bayonets.'

During the campaign on Saipan a Japanese detachment was cut off by the US 25th Marines. Gradually it was driven back and cornered in the south-

Extravagant promises by Tokyo of naval and air reinforcements could no longer blind him to reality. And what he planned was in short a Banzai in the grand manner. Either he would break the American attack or the whole of the remaining Japanese garrison would perish in the attempt.

'The barbarous attack of the enemy is being continued' he wrote in a final order of the day to his troops, 'we are dying without avail under the violent shelling and bombing . . . Whether we attack or whether we stay where we are there is only death. However, in death there is life. We must utilise this opportunity to exalt true Japanese manhood. I will advance with those who remain, to deliver still another blow to the American Devils, and leave my bones on Saipan as a bulwark of the Pacific.' Once again Japanese soldiers were instructed to dedicate themselves to the 'Seven lives to repay our country' theme which had been given to the detachment trying to break out earlier. But on this occasion there was no tactical objective: the attack was to be the largest mass-suicide yet staged in the Pacific. To make sure that his troops would be concentrated in sufficient time Saito laid his plans well in advance. The only way he had of communicating with most of his units was by means of runners and these were sent out three days beforehand. The orders were for every available man to rendezvous at a designated spot near the village of Makunsho, where the scorched fields of sugarcane were still thick enough to conceal the troops forming for the attack. The runners were compelled to make their way to the outlying units at night and it proved impossible for them to reach everybody. It was also inevitable that one of their despatches should fall into American hands. In consequence the Marines were aware that an attack was pending although it was not known exactly where it would break or from which direction it would come.

Once the message had been issued General Saito sat down to eat what was left of the more delectable Japanese rations; sake and canned crabmeat. Then, after the traditional ceremonies associated with this last supper, he said farewell to his staff and sat down outside his headquarters facing in the general direction of the Emperor's palace. A ceremonial sword was handed to him, and as soon as he had made the circumscribed incision in his stomach his adjutant – acting on prearranged orders – shot him through the head. (His body was recovered subsequently by the Marines and buried with full military honours.)

Command of the actual attack devolved upon Colonel Suzuki of the

Left and below: **Result of the suicidal charges on Saipan. Nearly 24,000 Japanese die, many in 'banzai' attacks which are repeated in spite of terrible losses**

135th Infantry. Exactly how many participated in it, the Japanese never could be sure. But from the evidence of the numbers of bodies subsequently buried, it appears that the attack force numbered about 3,000. The advance started from Makunsho about 0400 hours on the morning of 8th July 1944. Moving in formation down the narrow-gauge railway which ran near the shore the Japanese brushed aside the American outposts, and engaged two battalions of the 105th US Infantry shortly after 0500. In a screaming mass they charged, shouting 'Banzai, Banzai' – high pitched, blood curdling, words loaded with fanaticism, savagery and hate. The impetus of the initial charge was enough to carry them straight through the Americans; there was no stopping so many men whose only thought was to kill or be killed. The American artillery pounded the area from which the attack was developing, but it was ineffective where the actual fighting was taking place because the gunners could not shoot for fear of hitting their own people.

By 0600 the situation was one of chaotic confusion. The two American battalions had been shattered and savage fighting swirled about a dozen isolated pockets of American resistance. Some were overrun; some held out. Some of the Americans escaped into the hills; others near the shore were driven to the sea. Meanwhile, as the Japanese drove on, observers in the hills above the battlefield saw a strange phenomenon through their field-glasses. Behind the first lines of Japanese assault troops moved a weird procession: the lame, the sick and the halt. The wounded had left the hospitals and come out to die. Men in bandages, some on crutches, walking wounded helping each other along; some armed, some with only a bayonet or a grenade; many with no weapons at all were struggling up to try to kill a few Americans and then die in battle. Later it was found that some 300 patients too weak to move

had been killed by the Japanese themselves.

About a thousand yards behind where Saito's men had broken through, the American gunners fired their weapons at point-blank range as the Japanese surged towards them. Many of the seething mass died here before the gunners themselves were overrun. But by now the charge had lost its impetus, and when another American battalion rushed up to counterattack the great Banzai was over and it was the American's turn to attack. Nightfall found only two pockets of stubborn resistance and these were mopped up the following day.

The carnage had been ghastly beyond belief. Burial parties needed days to cope with the number of dead. One observer visiting the scene described exhausted US soldiers and Marines lying down to sleep among already rotting corpses because there was no place in the area that was free of the dead. As regards its only conceivable object, suicide, General Saito's Banzai had been an unqualified success.

The campaign was over soon after that – although here and there a handful of Japanese who had missed the Banzai for one reason or another tried to fight and died miserably in their holes. Others fled before the advance, ran to the edge of the cliffs that dropped away from the plateau and struggled down to the shore. Here was enacted the crowning horror of the whole battle. Some hundreds of civilians had taken refuge on the northern shore, and in caves in the cliffs which faced it. Now, believing themselves to have reached the last extremity they set about a veritable orgy of self-destruction. Mothers and fathers cut the throats of babies and strangled their children, and then hurled the tiny bodies off the cliff before jumping after them. Japanese soldiers lined up and waited patiently for their officers to hack off their heads. Three women were seen to join

hands and walk slowly into the sea until it covered them. Another, naked and in the last stages of childbirth, waded in after them to drown herself too. All this was in plain view of the US Marines on top of the beach. Men hardened in one of the bloodiest campaigns of the Pacific turned away from the sight, sick at heart and physically ill.

Surrender pleas were largely in vain. These people had been told that the Americans would kill them, and when a few of the miserable creatures responded to an American exhortation to surrender, they were shot down by Japanese soldiers in their midst or others still holed up in caves in the cliff face. One Japanese soldier was seen to shoot one by one a group of about fifteen women and children, pausing systematically to reload his rifle, and capping the performance by blowing himself up with a grenade. For all practical purposes the campaign on Saipan ended at this point – although thousands of armed and

Despite their stunning losses many Japanese still lurk on Saipan

suicidal Japanese still lurked in the jungle. For weeks afterwards they were being hunted out and killed, often at the rate of more than a hundred a day, in one of the biggest mopping up operations in history. When a count was taken in August nearly 24,000 Japanese soldiers had perished – many of them in suicidal gestures.

On Guam there was another Banzai charge which made history. At that time the Americans were holding a front of 2,000 yards, with a single division. On the night of 25th July 1944 it rained heavily and early on the morning of the 26th shells began to fall on the American positions. The staccato rattle of machine gun fire and the dull thump of bursting grenades then blended into the noise in a vicious night attack. The Japanese had decided to hurl the American Marines off Guam and back into the sea. Carrying land mines and explo-

Above: Cautious Marines advance inland on Guam. *Right:* The carnage of the futile Japanese 'banzai' attacks on Guam

sive charges on their belts the Japanese charged forwards screaming in English. (One war correspondent who was caught in the middle of the battle swore later that he heard them shouting 'One, two, three; you can't catch me!') The Marines fought back, but sheer weight of numbers took the Japanese through the thinly held perimeter. The position was stabilised eventually, but for some hours it was touch-and-go and for days after the Banzai attack had been broken up, parties and individual Japanese were being hunted down behind the front the Americans had re-established.

Two things distinguished this 'Banzai' from others. First was the careful reconnaissance that preceded the attack, and secondly the choice of where the breakthrough would be made. Patrols probed the American line until they were certain they had found its weakest point. Then, when they had established where the luckless defenders were dug in, they were ready for their attack. They chose to strike at a sector which they correctly concluded was held by the weakest US unit. At the very centre of the whole beachhead line no more than 250 men manned a position that ran for more than 2,000 yards – a frontage normally requiring about 600 men.

The signal for the attack appears to have been an orange flare which shot up from the Japanese lines seconds after a devastating mortar barrage had started to crash down on the American positions. A singsong voice shouted into the night and an avalanche of screaming forms bounded forward. With their bayonets gleaming in the light of the flames that went up over the battlefield the Japanese charged forward throwing grenades and howling 'Ban-zai-ai'. On the right and left of the US line the attack was held, for as fast as the Emperor's men advanced they were mowed down by automatic rifles and machine guns. In the centre the assault engulfed the isolated foxholes which made up the front-line, and focused on a hollow where some American tanks were parked. As the Japanese bore down on the tanks like a swarm of ants, the tanks fired their 75s at the charging masses. Many of the attackers were blown to bits but some of the survivors clambered up and over the steel monsters in a vain attempt to get at the crews inside. Others streamed past the tanks down a ravine which led to the beach. In front of them parties of US Marines tried to stem the rush and reform a front line. The night was hideous with explosions, lights and screams.

Action around the US heavy machine guns was typical of what happened. A Japanese grenade hit one gun, temporarily putting it out of action and its members saw the Japanese charge straight up to the barrel of the other – one Japanese soldier throwing himself over the muzzle in a gesture designed to permit his comrades to fulfill their role as well as take him to Yasukuni. The American crew were bayoneted and the Japs tried to lift the entire gun on its mount and turn it round. One of the US Marines blasted them with his automatic rifle and the Japanese dropped the gun. Three others remained and when the Marine turned his fire on them one was seen to pull out a grenade, hold it to his head and blow himself up. Minutes later another party of Japanese appeared. Again, several paused at the gun and tried to swing it round. They had almost succeeded when from the darkness a lone Japanese soldier raced headlong towards them, tripped over a body several feet away and flew through the air. There was a blinding flash as he literally blew apart. He had been a human

Above and below: 'When it was properly light, bulldozers and burial squads found some 800 Japanese dead'; the culmination of the horrific night 'banzai' on Guam in July 1944. *Right:* US troops search out the enemy

The American assault on Iwo Jima against General Kuribayashi's strongly defended positions

bomb, carrying a land mine and a blast charge on his waist.

Three hours after the attack had begun the Japanese had reached the hill overlooking the beachhead. Their objective was in sight and the decimated rabble which remained was hurriedly pushed into line for the final *Banzai*. Buched together, howling and stumbling, the first wave lowered their bayonets and swept on to be chopped down by the concentrated fire of fresh Marines who were grimly awaiting their mad rush. Some of the Japanese had been wounded already and they were swathed in grey bandages. But they all swept forward when their officers gave the command. And they died to a man. Only a few scattered individuals who had not got as far as the hill now remained to be mopped up.

When it was properly light bull-

dozers and burial squads found some 800 Japanese. Many others were killed or sealed in caves. In effect this particular suicidal charge had wasted the cream of the Japanese troops on Guam. When it failed they had nothing more to oppose the Americans. Over the next few weeks they continued to launch smaller attacks, but their offensive power was broken.

The Americans now pushed inland and there were some desperate moments among the wooded hills and valleys. In many places the hills were steep coral formations that afforded the Japanese numerous caves in which to hide. Calls to surrender rarely brought any response and security had to be bought with flame-throwers and thermite grenades. For the Japanese who remained on Guam the only alternative to defeat was death. This they accepted was their lot, and whenever they got a chance to reorganize the Americans were made grimly aware of the fact.

In Malaya, in Burma, and on the far-

cement. General Kuribayashi had had plenty of time to prepare his defences and the result was a series of pillboxes and strong points linked by a prodigious chain of tunnels. Entire hills had been hollowed out and hundreds of caves and recesses connected up to provide hiding places and shelters for the defenders.

Kuribayashi knew that an attack was coming and he had prepared his men spiritually as well as physically for the ordeal. Morale generally must have presented him with quite a problem long before the fighting commenced. As has been remarked already, the Japanese soldier was a long-suffering individual unaccustomed to much in the way of comfort and recreation. But garrison life on Iwo Jima was pretty grim even for the Japanese. Yet the portly little general managed to infuse much of his own grim determination into his men, and copies of the 'Courageous Battle Vows' which he had printed and issued were found on many of the Japanese dead when the Americans finally overran their positions:

'Above all we shall dedicate ourselves and our entire strength to the defence of this island.

'We shall grasp bombs, charge enemy tanks and destroy them.

'We shall infiltrate into the midst of the enemy and annihilate them.

'With every salvo we will without fail kill the enemy.

'Each man will make it his duty to kill ten of the enemy before dying.

'Until we are destroyed to the last man we shall harass the enemy with guerilla tactics.'

A thorough realist in military matters, Kuribayashi was determined to capitalize to the full on the suicide weapon. His battle vows were implemented by more tangible oaths, taken by individual men, to volunteer for death or glory missions in the island's defence. Special scarves issued to all such volunteers were worn proudly around their heads. Often entire units volunteered en masse.

flung islands of the Pacific theatre, wherever Japanese troops were required to serve the Emperor, the story was the same. Japanese commanders could always count on Japan's greatest military asset – the willingness of most of her men to die. On Iwo Jima, 660 air miles from Tokyo as the US bombers flew, the general officer commanding the garrison was a certain Lieutenant-General Tasamichi Kuribayashi. And according to the Japanese press Kuribayashi was a short, squat, brown man of fifty-four, 'whose slightly protuberant belly is full of fine fighting spirit.' But fighting spirit was not Kuribayashi's only quality, for he was also an able tactician and a good soldier. Moreover he was determined to capitalize on the suicidal qualities of his troops. Iwo Jima was a volcanic island covering eight square miles and shaped like a pork chop. The beaches and most of the soil consisted of a strange volcanic ash, which could be turned into a granite-like concrete when mixed with

Above: US Marines try to locate Iwo Jima's defenders. *Below:* American tanks, equipped with flame-throwers, attempt to dislodge the Japanese

Above: A grenade on a suspected Japanese position was often the best answer
Below: There were always isolated pockets of resistance that needed handling

Not that the general had any intention of throwing lives away needlessly. A score of examples of Banzai had convinced him of its futility in the face of American firepower and he made it clear to all ranks that when suicide tactics were called for, they were aimed at accomplishing some definite constructive purposes. There was to be no retreat and no surrender, but no counterattacks were to be staged until the Japanese positions had been over-run.

The Japanese played their cards craftily and the three weeks which it took to break the back of their defences made Iwo Jima one of the bloodiest operations the Americans had ever undertaken. Time after time during the course of that three weeks the invaders thought that they had stunned the Japanese with a devasting barrage from their supporting warships. And time and again the Japanese let them walk into an ambush, and then showed that they had lived through that terrible fire. Small groups of men on Kuribayashi's suicide missions repeatedly infiltrated through the American lines, reoccupying positions that had been overrun, to fire on the rear of the assault troops.

The Americans advanced, but every step was made at an appalling cost, and the conquest of Iwo Jima was a grim struggle of attrition. But the strain told on the Japanese also, and as the campaign roared through its second week Kuribayashi began to realize that he could not win. Where was the Imperial Navy and the Japanese Air Force, he asked in a radio signal to his chiefs in Tokyo? In fact most of the Japanese navy was at the bottom of the sea by this time, and what was left of the Japanese Air Force could not break through the powerful screening fire which guarded the US expeditionary force on Iwo.

'Fight to the death, if necessary keeping the last round for yourself' Many did

On 9th March American Marines finally completed the operation which has been designed to smash through Kuribayashi's main defence line. The campaign was far from over since so many of the Japanese strong points had been bypassed. These remained to plague the Americans' rear, as did hundreds of other Japanese holed up among the ridges and ravines in caves and connected by tortuous underground passages. The Japanese reacted to the breakthrough with one of their counterattacks. It was not in fact ordered by General Kuribayashi, for it turned out later that he was penned up in a cave some distance from the scene of the action and was completely out of touch with his troops. Perhaps these men decided that as their positions had been overrun their general would expect them to comply with the original orders. Or perhaps they simply felt that the show was

over and that they were supposed to sell their lives as dearly as possible. Whichever was the case they sallied forth.

What transpired could not be counted a Banzai charge. Indeed what was attempted was not so much a charge as a mass infiltration effort, aimed less at smashing the US front than at breaking through to disrupt the more vulnerable rear access: blowing up supply dumps, tanks, motor transport, artillery, even planes if they could manage to get through to the airfields. But it was definitely a suicidal operation. The men, loaded down with grenades, demolition charges and assorted explosives obviously never expected to survive. Very few of them did.

Most of the action took place at night in the area held by the US 23rd Marines. Kuribayashi's men used machine guns, mortars and such artillery as remained to them, and the US guns responded by plastering the areas through which the Japanese must advance. The usual nightmare scene developed, and throughout the night there was some fierce hand-to-hand fighting. But dawn found the infiltrators scattered and bogged down, their position hopeless. They had not accomplished anything of tactical importance. Some blew themselves up; many others had to be eliminated in a slow and painful mopping up operation. What happened to Kuribayashi nobody knows. Reports had it that he was holed up with a powerful detachment of do-or-die individuals. And one Japanese who was captured alive declared that the general had organized and led a final Banzai. However a careful examination of the bodies, swords and documents found on the dead failed to confirm this.

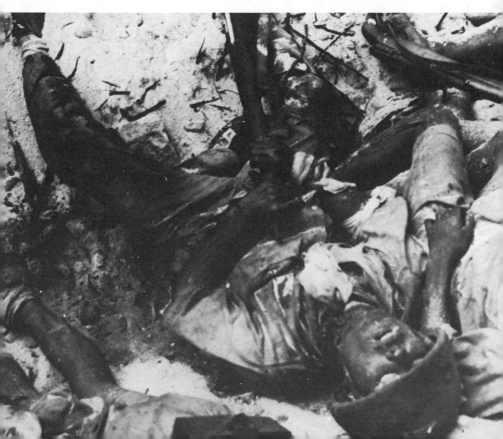

The human
torpedoes

Japanese suicide tactics were not confined to operations on land; at sea there were men who also deliberately accepted annihilation in the hope of defeating the Allies.

In 1922 the Washington Naval Disarmament Conference ruled that Japan's capital ships would be restricted to sixty per cent of the total allowed to the United States or Britain. Distressed by this decision, senior naval officers in the Emperor's Imperial Navy looked for means to overcome the limitation. In consequence an intense modernisation plan was initiated and new weapons were developed; among the latter was a remarkable new torpedo. In the 'twenties and early 'thirties the naval strategies of all the major powers revolved round the dominant role of the battleship and quantitative superiority was measured by the numbers of these capital ships. To restore the balance between Japan's navy and the fleets of the two Western Powers, a new weapon was needed which had a greater range than the guns of the British and American battleships. Because the new torpedo could do this it went further than equalising the disparity forced on Japan; it also provided an opportunity for a revolution in surface actions.

The steam-driven torpedoes with which the navies of all the maritime powers were equipped had by this time attained the peak of their performance. Some attempts had been made by Britain and France to develop new propulsion systems, but nothing had come of them. Oxygen had been considered but the idea had been given up as too dangerous. Realizing that this gas in a torpedo propulsion system offered a far greater range and speed, the Japanese quietly set to work to develop it, and in 1933 Vice-Admiral Toshihide Asaguma and Rear Admiral Kaneji Kishimoto received special rewards from the Emperor for their work in this field. No details were published but it was learned later that they had produced a giant torpedo 24 inches in diameter, nearly 30 feet long and weighing 6,000 pounds. This weapon, called the 'Type 93' by the designers because it was perfected 2,593 years after the founding of the Japanese Empire and became known later as 'The Long Lance', carried a 1,000 pound high explosive warhead. The latter was about twice as much as that carried in American and British torpedoes. Asaguma and Kishimoto had done all that was expected of them, and had it not been for the advent of aerial tactics as the primary striking power in naval actions these torpedoes could have maintained Japan's naval supremacy throughout the war.

In due course all Japanese destroyers and cruisers were equipped with mounts for Type 93 torpedoes, and the bulky oxygen-producing equipment that was needed for them was installed. Needless to say, this process was shrouded in secrecy, and the oxygen generators were explained away as special air-conditioners. During February 1942, at the battle of the Java Sea, the Long Lances were used in action for the first time. The result was a shattering success against a combined force of US, British, Dutch and Australian warships. But the success was shortlived, and as the Imperial Navy lost the ships which carried the new weapons into battle, the torpedoes remained to collect dust in the Imperial Navy's Ordnance Depots.

Japan's concern for submarines also stemmed from the 1922 Washington Conference since it was reckoned that submarines, like torpedoes, could help to even out the disparity that had been forced upon Japan. By December 1941 sixty-four giant 'I' class submarines were ready for action, and twenty midget submarines had also been built. Deriving originally from the 'human torpedoes' which had been used by the Japanese during the Russo-Japanese war these curious little craft carried two men and were capable of remaining submerged for five hours. They were not weapons of suicide in the true sense of the word, although manning them inevitably entailed a considerable risk to their crew. Each of the midgets was carried into action by one of the giant 'I' class submarines which had to surface in order to release its charge. After the mission the same submarine was supposed to recover them. However, in their first action at Pearl Harbor it was soon seen that there was little chance of this being effected. Nevertheless the Japanese temperament was ideally suited to the calls for doubtful missions of this type, and there was no shortage of volunteers.

Meantime plans were being concocted for a one-man midget which could be released while the mother submarine was submerged. During the winter of 1942-43 two naval officers, lieutenants Nishina and Kuroki, and a naval architect Hiroshi Suzukawa drafted a design based on the Type 93 Long Lance. All the major components of the original torpedo were retained, and the only major modification was the inclusion of an additional section between the warhead in the nose and the oxygen motor. This was the pilot's compartment, fitted with a periscope and a set of controls enabling a man to direct the torpedo run. By the spring of 1943 the designers had completed their drawings, and had calculated that their 'manned' torpedo, fitted with a 3,000 pound high explosive warhead, would have a range of forty nautical miles. The Long Lance had already proved it could break the back of a heavy cruiser; with a man to direct it and a warhead three times more powerful there was every reason to suppose it could do the same to a battleship or an aircraft carrier.

Things had already started to go badly for the Imperial Navy and the Naval General Staff in Tokyo were looking for some way of changing the pattern of the Pacific war. The plans were presented for what the designers were now calling the *kaiten*. (The literal translation of *kaiten* is 'Heaven Shaker'. But in Japanese it means much more – suggesting a radical change in affairs.) But they were rejected as being too fantastic even for consideration. But when the Imperial Navy's attempt to smash the Americans at Saipan went awry the men in Tokyo began to have second thoughts about the *kaiten*. Nishina and Kuroki's persistent pleas to the Navy Ministry had culminated in a petition written in their own blood. It is doubtful if this had much effect; what undoubtedly caused the Naval General Staff to listen was what the Americans termed the 'Marianas Turkey Shoot.' when over 400 Japanese planes were lost. Thirteen months after they first sought it,

Two-man submarines were adapted for suicide missions

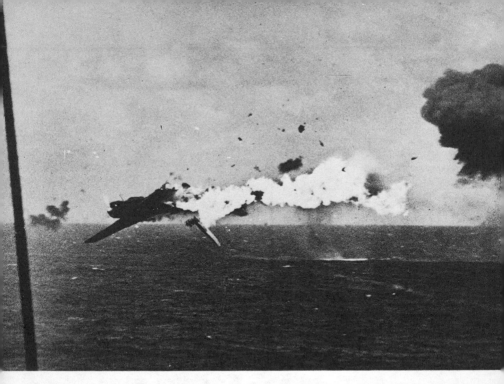

**Yorktown destroys a torpedo plane.
Japanese air power is waning**

permission was given for the construction of a prototype. But only on condition that it should have an escape hatch giving the *kaiten* pilot a chance to get away safely once he had put his weapon on a sure course to the target. In February 1944 the prototype was approved and a base was set up on Otsujima Island near the Kure naval base, headquarters of Japan's Sixth Fleet and submarine force.

Strict security measures kept news of the project out of the public eye and only a few *kaiten* had been built by June 1944. But when the extent of the disaster which had overtaken the Imperial Navy in the Marianas finally dawned on them, the Naval General Staff sent out a frantic order for more to be produced on a crash priority. A second order called for volunteers to operate a *Kyukoko heiki*, a new national salvation weapon, on missions from which they were not expected to return alive. At first no mention was made of the nature of the weapon, but even when it was learned that their probable fate was an unseen death beneath the waves there were plenty of volunteers. Indeed it appears that the first ones were grateful at being accepted. Selection was supposedly based on three qualifications: physical and moral strength, evidence of strong sense of patriotism, and a minimum of family responsibilities. Married men were excluded and very few elder or only sons were chosen. The accent was on young fit men who would have little tendency to look over their shoulders.

At the *kaiten* depot on Otsushima, 'Base P', every effort was made to instill *esprit de corps, Yamato damashii,* Japanese spirit, in the volunteers. On arrival they were introduced to a prototype of their steel coffins before being shown to their quarters. The latter were, like their food, luxurious in comparison with what most of

58

them had known in their previous training. But there were few recreation facilities – no cinema and no women. Nor were the men permitted leave of absence until they had completed their training, and were ready for the mission which was to be their finale.

Nishina and Kuroki organised the training of the first volunteers. But on 6th September, 1944, the *kaiten* claimed its first victim when Kuroki's torpedo stuck in the mud at the bottom of the placid waters of the Inland Sea. Six other lives were to be lost in training before the end of the war brought the demise of the *kaiten*. But, from September 1944 until the end of the Okinawa campaign, volunteers in groups which were given traditional names such as 'God's warriors', 'Group for the furtherance of the *Samurai* way', took *kaiten* courses at Otsushima. Lessons in the functions of the Type 93 torpedo were followed by simulated dry run missions to familiarise the pilots with the controls and accustom them to the confined space of their tiny cabin. Submerged practice drill against ships moored in Tokuyama Bay followed. Finally, when the pilots were considered proficient at these drills, the group was embarked on one of the fleet submarines for an operational dummy run.

Each of the I class submarines fitted to carry *kaiten* could take six of the weapons. During the approach to the target the *kaiten* pilots climbed into their tiny craft through a special hatch which was then sealed off. As the submarine closed on its victim, a telephone link between the submarine's conning tower and the *kaiten* enabled the captain to keep the pilots informed on the relative positions of the target. At the optimum moment the *kaiten*'s engines were started and they were released at five-second intervals from the mother ship. Once in motion the pilot could observe the target through his own periscope, and make the necessary corrections to his course. Then at about 500 yards distance he would switch his craft on to automatic control for the final dash at full speed submerged to a depth of about twelve feet.

Inside the *kaiten* even a small man was cramped. And, although the controls were simple, considerable skill was needed to operate the craft efficiently. Under his feet was a tiny box of emergency rations and a small flask of Japanese whiskey. Neither was intended for operational missions. Directly in front of the pilot's face was the viewing glass of the short, stubby periscope which was raised or lowered by a crank on the right. Also on the right but above the pilot's head was the valve regulating the oxygen flow to the motor immediately behind him. Overhead on the left was a lever connected with the *kaiten*'s diving planes, which controlled the rate of descent or climb underwater. Below this lever was a valve for letting in sea water. This was necessary to maintain stability as the oxygen fuel was used up. Finally, there was the rudder control lever which steered the weapon right or left and which was the last control to be touched by the pilot when he set his final course for an enemy ship. To operate the *kaiten* efficiently a man really needed six hands. And about the same number of eyes for watching the control panel. Apart from the periscope there was a gyrocompass, a clock, and depth and fuel gauges. Any sudden change in the controls or contact with an underwater obstacle invariably resulted in the pilot banging his head on one or other of the instruments. In consequence, bandaged heads were a frequent sight on Otsushima.

On an operational mission the captain of the mother submarine would align his ship with the target and each *kaiten* man would check his compass bearing. In the conning tower the attack course of each individual *kaiten* would then be plotted and relayed by telephone. For example a

An experimental version of the *kaiten* is launched

typical order might be 'Go right thirty degrees on leaving. Speed twenty-five knots for twelve minutes and thirty seconds.' These instructions were designed to bring the *kaiten* to within 500 yards of his target, at which point the pilot was expected to raise his periscope and set the controls for his dash for the enemy ship's vitals at the top speed of forty knots.

Training finished with the successful completion of an operational dummy run. The *kaiten* men were then entitled to a few days leave before assignment to an operational mission. On this leave they were not expected to reveal the fact that they were now committed to a suicide operation. Nevertheless many of the families of such men appear to have guessed the reason for the special leave even if they were not told. Any suspicions they may have had would often be confirmed by little luxuries with which their relative was laden when he arrived. When the leave was over it was not considered good taste to mention that the next meeting would probably be at Yasukuni. But no doubt the thought was there.

When their leave expired, the *kaiten* men returned to duty at the submarine bases of either Otsushima or Hikari. Pending their assignment to a mission they were free at both places to consummate any last desires before they sailed off to certain death, and food, alcohol or women were theirs for the asking. Few of the doomed men are reported to have availed themselves of the sweets that were offered and most appear to have concentrated on setting their affairs in order. Wills were redrafted and last letters home were composed:

'I shall die . . . cherishing the conviction that Japan has been and will be a place where only lovely homes, brave women, and beautiful friendships are allowed to exist. . .'

Warheads destined for the nose sections of *kaiten*

'. . . May my death be as sudden and clean as the shattering of crystal. . . like cherry blossoms in the spring let us fall clean and radiant. . .'

'. . . Most important, do not weep for me. . .'

A party in honour of the six individuals allocated to an operational mission was usually organised on the night before they left Japan on what was expected to be their one way voyage. The admiral commanding the Imperial Submarine Fleet or his deputy was invariably the guest of honour, and this last supper would be the occasion for a good deal of sentimental outburst. Toasts would be drunk to Japan – God's Land Eternal, loyalty would be pledged to 'His Majesty Forever', and the *kaiten* men would vow to destroy the largest enemy ships they could find. The meal itself was made up of traditional Japanese festive dishes: *tai* (fish), dried seaweed, rice and *kachi kuri* (victory chestnuts). (These chestnuts are always served in Japan on occasions where wishes for success are the order of the day.) In the Japan of late 1944 there was a shortage of almost every kind of consumer goods. But at these parties canned fruit and other hard-to-get items were plentiful. *Sake* flowed freely, and the 'Warrior's Song' was sung over and over again:

'In serving on the seas, be a corpse saturated with water.'

'In serving on the land be a corpse covered with weeds.'

'. . . But we have nothing to regret so long as we die fighting for our Emperor.'

Tears were many, and the occasions could hardly be said to support the myth that the Japanese are an unemotional race.

Next morning, the *kaiten* men were expected to parade in new uniforms for the farewell ceremony. Their belongings had been packed ready to be sent home, and this luggage would include locks of hair and fingernail parings, so that relatives would have

**A *kaiten* suicide torpedo found by
the Americans at Ulithi Atoll**

'remains' for an honourable burial. On
a table covered with a white cloth six
short swords and six *hachimaki* would
be laid out. To Japanese fighting men
these swords were as symbolic as the
shields of ancient Sparta. Handing the
shield to her son a Spartan mother
would command him to return to her
'With it, or on it'. Victorious he would
come back carrying his shield, defeated he would be back on it dead.
Returning alive without it would
mean that he had discarded it in order
to be able to run away faster. The

short sword means the same thing in
Japan. A man must fight and win, or
use the short sword to commit *seppuku* – hara-kiri – in atonement for
his failure. Once the sword was presented the recipient's life was pledged
to the Emperor, either through battle,
death or disembowelment.

As each man's name was called out
he would step up to the table and
salute the admiral. In turn he would
bow and then present the *kaiten* man
with a sword and one of the *hachimaki*.
This was a replica of the cloth worn
centuries earlier by the *samurai* to
absorb perspiration and to keep their
long hair from falling into their eyes.

Saluting again, each *kaiten* pilot would step back into line and tie the *hachimaki* around his head. Written on each in graceful brush strokes would be a slogan appropriate to the name of the *kaiten* group – 'Reborn seven times to serve the nation', 'Loyalty to the Emperor for ever' or something similar. Shallow cups of water would then be passed around. These were for the death toast – water because a Japanese warrior facing death traditionally drank water not *sake* to signify purity of soul. Drinking this toast was the solemn climax to the ceremony. After it the *kaiten* group would march down to the pier from which they were to embark on their mission. En route they would stop and bow before a shrine specially constructed for *kaiten* men. Officers and men serving at Otsushima and Hikari invariably collected to see them off, and for the first mission there was a band to play '*Kimigayo*. . .' 'May Thy reign last one thousand, eight thousand generations. . .'

At the pier, photographs would be taken of the group holding their swords at the salute. Then into a launch to be taken to the fleet submarine, which was waiting to get underway. Another batch of human torpedoes was en route to Yasukuni.

Divine Wind

Ohnishi bids farewell to a group of
kamikaze pilots prior to their
attacking US ships in Leyte Gulf

occasions were not suicide attacks in
the true sense of the word since the
pilots in any case stood almost no
chance of survival. There were also a
few not fully authenticated reports of
individual pilots of both nations with
planes in perfect condition, deliberately diving into their targets. But
these were isolated cases of self-
sacrifice. The organised Kamikaze
attack was an entirely different
affair. In this operation the pilot, or
the entire crew, of an attacking
aircraft eliminated even the remotest
opportunity for survival once committed to the final dive against the enemy.
Death was the companion of the
Kamikaze pilot, just as it was of the
kaiten.

As the year 1944 drew to a close it
was evident to many of the Japanese
officers responsible for the day-to-day
prosecution of the war, that the
likelihood of victory was receding.
The Imperial Navy had been beaten
and dispersed, Japan's merchant shipping had been practically annihilated
and casualties had so reduced the
navy's pilots that there were not
enough to man Japan's remaining
aircraft carriers. By the beginning of
September 1944 all the air bases in
the Marianas and Caroline Islands and
along the north coast of New Guinea
were in the hands of the Americans.
Clearly it was now only a matter of
time before they launched the final
all-out assault against the Philippines. But before an invasion force
could be launched the airfields from
which Japanese bombers and fighters
could strike had to be knocked out.
Realising this the Japanese reinforced
their forward air bases in the Philippines. Following an attack by US
carrier-based aircraft on Davao, six
squadrons of Zero fighters were transferred from Clark Field on Luzon to
Cebu Island in the central Philippines.
They arrived too late to participate

'Kamikaze' is a word which has been
taken into the English language to
epitomize the suicidal act. Today it is
more usually associated with Tokyo's
taxi drivers than with the men of the
'Special Attack Corps' who, in the
words of Admiral Ohnishi, thought of
themselves as 'already gods without
earthly desires.' According to a
favourite Japanese legend, a 'divine
wind', a Kamikaze, was sent by the
sun Goddess to wreck the huge fleet of
the Mongol conqueror Kublai Khan
in 1281. 660 years later there was a call
for another divine wind to defeat an
enemy on Japan's doorstep. So it
seemed appropriate to call the men
who flew aerial versions of the *Banzai*
charge by the legendary name.

Contrary to the popular view, the
Kamikazes were not organised on the
spur of the moment. During many of
the earlier air battles both American
and Japanese pilots whose planes had
been hopelessly disabled attempted,
and several times succeeded, in crash
diving on enemy objectives. These

Above: US Air Force pounds the Japanese-held Clark Field. Right: Japanese aircraft caught on the ground

in Davao's defence, and it was assumed that the Americans had withdrawn their carriers to the open sea. Two days later, however, the American task force returned to within striking distance of Cebu and launched an attack which came as a complete surprise to the Japanese garrison. Over a hundred Zeros were caught on the Cebu runways and when the screaming Hellcats had finished their work more than fifty had been reduced to charred wreckage or blown to pieces. For the Japanese this was a disaster of the first magnitude; in a single stroke the Americans had destroyed nearly two thirds of Japan's entire fighter plane force in the Philippines.

In an attempt to counter the effects of this devastating attack, what remained of the Zeros were ordered back to Luzon and Manila, and all the replacements that could be spared were ordered to be sent to the Philippines. But before the shattered remains of Japan's air force in the

Philippines could be re-organized and rebuilt, the Americans struck again. When they had finished pounding the Philippines, Okinawa, and Formosa, the airfields there were left with a mere pile of burning, tangled wreckage.

It was not just a matter of losing planes, although that was serious enough. Naval pilots were in short supply and army pilots did not seem to be sufficiently experienced to cope with their American aerial adversaries. Suggestions were now voiced that the only way to halt the Americans would be by deliberately crash-diving Japanese bombers into the American carriers. This idea ultimately reached Admiral Soemu Toyota, Commander-in-Chief of the Imperial Navy's Combined Fleet. But it was not until a report was circulated that Rear Admiral Arima, the commander of the 26th Air Flotilla at Manila, had deliberately crashed his plane into an American warship that Toyota consented to the creation of a do-and-die organisation.

Arima may therefore be credited with making a notable contribution to Japan's suicidal tactics. Precise and formal by nature, but slim and unprepossessing in appearance, he came from an old Samurai family and he was dedicated to professionalism. On Manila he preferred to live in a frugal style, and to spend most of his time at Nichols Field maintaining a close supervision of the operations of his command. On 15th October when an American task force was sighted off Luzon, Arima was at this airfield. And when the decision was taken to strike at the American armada with every available Japanese plane, it appears that Arima suddenly announced that he would lead the attack in person.

Followed by twelve bombers and eighty-six Zeros, he took off about 3pm. The American fleet was spotted about an hour later and Arima's last message paraphrased an order by Japanese high command. 'The destiny of the homeland depends on this battle. Everyone is expected to do his best.' Minutes later a section of the wing of his aircraft struck the flight deck of the carrier *Franklin*. Arima's fellow pilots subsequently said that he led the way into the attack by crash diving on an American warship, variously identified as a destroyer, a cruiser, and a carrier. As Arima did not survive, his intentions could never be verified. But it is presumed that the debris which ended up on the *Franklin* came from his plane. It is possible that Arima never intended a dramatic finale, that his purpose was merely to set an example and stiffen the determination of his pilots to press their attack home, and

that a one-way mission was not in his thoughts. Whether this was so or not, the fact remains that his action was seen as a response to the high command's call for duty. And the result was a climax as violent as the circumstances which engendered it.

Although the decision to form what amounted to an airborne suicide corps may be attributed to Arima's dramatic gesture there had already been some discussion among naval air crews about the possibilities of crash-diving tactics. Much of this was inspired not so much by the Battle of the Philippine Sea (normally referred to by the Japanese as the Marianas Sea Battle) in which three Japanese carriers went to the bottom, as by the marked increase in flying training accidents. Almost daily men were killed in practice landings and take-offs from carrier decks. Seeing this the pilots themselves began to believe that if they were going to die on carrier decks it would be better to do so in crashes on those of the enemy. And if the planes contained bombs, the American ships would be sunk at the same time. In due course this talk led Rear Admiral Sueo Obayashi, commander of the 3rd Carrier Division, and Captain Eiichiro Iyo, captain of the carrier *Chiyoda*, to suggest the idea of a Special Attack Force to Admiral Ozawa.

But it was not Ozawa who was to be the man directly responsible for the formation of the Kamikazes. On 17th October a new naval commander had arrived at Manila to take over the First Air Fleet. This was Vice-Admiral Kakijiro Ohnishi, the man who had been instrumental in drawing up the Yamamoto plan for the attack on Pearl Harbor, and who with Yamamoto had been largely responsible for the build-up of the Imperial Navy's Fleet Air Arm. Ohnishi was a headstrong arrogant individual who exuded a masculinity and drive contagious

Aerial view of the bomb damage after the Formosa raids

to the younger men who served with him, and obnoxious to his equals and seniors. Many junior naval officers worshipped Ohnishi, just as most senior officers detested him for his aggressive, showy manners and the condescension he displayed towards those who disagreed with him. But no-one could dispute his experience or zeal. As a pilot he had seen a good deal of distinguished service in China, as chief of staff to the Commander of the Navy Land Based Air Force, he had proved himself to be a capable staff officer. Ohnishi was good, and he knew it.

He arrived at Manila at a critical time. An American task force had been spotted and this was seen as a clear indication that the Americans were about to make their all-out bid for the Philippines. Admiral Toyota had ordered every Japanese warship in the entire Philippines area to steam as quickly as possible to the south eastern area of the island waters and to assemble in battle formation. They were to be joined by almost every other fighting ship of the Imperial Navy. Nine battleships, including the giants *Yamato* and *Musashi*, eleven heavy cruisers, six light cruisers, thirty-eight destroyers, and four carriers were to join them from Singapore, Formosa and Hiroshima Bay. As the Americans were known to have many aircraft-carriers off Leyte some means had to be found to immobilize them while the Japanese battleships closed in to annihilate the remainder of the US task force.

Everything depended on Ohnishi's ability to deal with the American carriers. Yet his hands were literally tied before he made his first move. By scraping every available airfield on the islands he could muster no more than thirty serviceable Zero fighters, and a similar number of patched up Type 1 Betty bombers. For the coming operations he had a pitiful total of only sixty planes. Ohnishi realized the futility of his task: that not even by the wildest stretch of the imagina-

Admiral Soemu Toyoda

tion could he hope, by orthodox methods, to destroy the American carriers so well guarded by their Hellcat fighters. Yet if he failed to destroy them, Ohnishi mused, even the mighty *Yamato* and *Musashi* could be sunk before they even saw the American fleet, let alone engaged it in combat.

On the morning of 19th October Ohnishi presented himself at Toyoda's headquarters with a proposal that crash-dive tactics should be employed in support of the forthcoming naval action. There was still a great reluctance to accept that suicidal attacks would be the most effective way of fighting. But Ohnishi's persuasive dominance, coupled with the realisation that the outcome of the war would be decided once and for all by this operation *Sho*, eventually carried the meeting. '*Sho*' means Victory. The plan for this operation was drawn up in July 1944 when the Americans had broken through Japan's defence line in New Guinea and the Marianas. Designed as an 'offensive-defensive' to counter the next American offensives, Operation Victory was another attempt to precipitate the 'decisive' naval battle which had been the

cornerstone of Japanese naval strategy. The decision to activate it was taken when it appeared that the Americans had selected the Philippines as their next objective, and were concentrating at Leyte.

Admiral Teraoka, Ohnishi's predecessor as commander of the First Air Fleet, was present at the discussions and he recorded the following bizarre comments:

'Ordinary tactics are ineffective'.

'We must be superhuman in order to win the war.'

'Volunteers for suicide missions will have to be reported to Imperial Headquarters before their take-off, so that they will feel secure and composed.'

'Should we speak directly to the young fliers or through their group commanders?'

'It would be better for future actions to have their group commanders present the proposition.'

'If the first suicide unit is organised by fighter pilot volunteers, other units will follow their example. If all air units do it, surface units will also be inclined to take part. And if there is a unanimous response by the Navy, the Army will follow suit.'

In the event, it was decided to let Ohnishi handle the arrangements for recruiting the first units.

Ohnishi left Toyoda's headquarters shortly before noon and as soon as he got back to his own headquarters a message was sent to Mabalacat, summoning the commanding officer of the 201st Air Group, Captain Sakae Yamamoto, and his adjutant, Commander Tadashi Nakajima, to Manila. But by 4pm, when neither had arrived, Ohnishi could contain his impatience no longer and he set off for Mabalacat hoping to meet them en route. Yamamoto had waited to see the operational sortie on its way, and somehow or other the two cars travelling in opposite directions missed each other. Two men met Ohnishi when he drove to the main headquarters of the Mabalacat airfield: Asaicki Tamai,

Admiral Isoroku Yamamoto

the executive officer of the air base, and Commander Rikihei Inoguchi, senior staff officer of the First Air Fleet. Inside the headquarters Ohnishi soberly outlined his plan: 'As you know the war situation is grave. The appearance of strong American forces in Leyte Gulf has been confirmed. . . Our surface forces are already in motion. . . we must hit the enemy's carriers and keep them neutralized for at least one week.' Then Ohnishi broached his momentous idea: 'In my opinion there is only one way of assuring that our meagre strength will be effective to a maximum degree. That is to organize suicide attack units composed of Zero fighters armed with 250-kilogram bombs, each plane to crash-dive into an American carrier. . . What do you think?' There it was, the bold desperate plan to stem the tide. And the way it was put across was worthy of the violent man who was given to violent decisions.

According to Inoguchi, both he and Tamai were momentarily stunned, and to gain time Tamai sent for the armament officer to ask what the effect would be of a plane carrying a 250-kilogram bomb smashing into a carrier's flight deck. The arma-

ment officer replied that it would probably take several days to repair the damage. Moreover a deliberate attempt to crash bodily into the carrier would have a better chance of success than any of the conventional bombing techniques then in vogue. The answer was precisely what Tamai had expected. But he was not prepared to accept sole responsibility for ordering his subordinates to commit suicide. Turning to Ohnishi, he said: 'I cannot decide a matter of this gravity. It must be referred to my CO, Captain Yamamoto.' Ohnishi's reply was curt. He had spoken to Yamamoto on the telephone, he said, and Yamamoto had delegated the responsibility to Tamai; it was now up to the executive officer to say whether or not the 201st Air Group would form a crash-dive unit. Since no further prevarication was possible Tamai asked permission to consult the flight commanders in private. Ohnishi nodded, and when Tamai returned to the room twenty minutes later it was to say that he would organise a suicide unit without further delay. Having spoken to some of the pilots, he could assure the admiral that the unit would not lack volunteers.

The next move was again up to Tamai. From the motley collection of young pilots in the 201st Air Group he had to select volunteers for the suicidal missions which would be ordered within the next few days. All of them were inexperienced, and few were officers. But their morale was high, and when Tamai addressed a hastily called parade to tell them what was proposed they responded enthusiastically. The precarious position of the Japanese fleet and air groups in the Philippines was already well understood, and the pilots knew that the chances of staving off the anticipated assault were slender. They also appreciated that the odds were heavily weighted against their own survival. In such circumstances a patriotic appeal could hardly fail to

gain their support. Twenty-three non-commissioned officers volunteered for the first assignment, and all that remained was to select the officer who was to lead them.

At this point the first name that came into Tamai's mind was that of Naoshi Kanno. Lieutenant Kanno was a colourful character with a reputation for dare-devil fearlessness. Three months previously he had successfully rammed a American B-24 with his Zero, and by some lucky chance survived. Since then he had demonstrated his skill at skip bombing practice – skimming low over the sea and bouncing a 250-kilogram bomb on the water into the side of a target with the same effect as a torpedo. In short he possessed all the expected qualities of leadership which would appeal to men embarking on an airborne *banzai*. But Kanno was away in Japan, collecting Zeros and reinforcements to replace the casualties at Davao. The next best of those who were available was Lieutenant Yukio Seki, a twenty-three year old regular officer who had joined the 201st Air Group less than a month before. Seki was a quiet, earnest individual who had not particularly distinguished himself since he joined the group. He was also a married man. But he was known to have a strong sense of patriotism, and when Tamai asked him if he was prepared to command the unorthodox 'attack unit', Seki jumped at the opportunity.

One question which now remained to be settled was what this particular suicide corps should be called. When Inoguchi suggested '*Shimpu*' (another way of reading the characters for 'Kamikaze') Tamai agreed. 'We need a man-made Kamikaze', he said. Ohnishi also approved, and thus it was that the first twenty four volunteers became the *Shimpu* Attack Corps, of four sections: *Shikishima,*

A young kamikaze pilot with Samurai sword before his one-way mission

Yamato, Asahi and Yamazakura—names from a well known poem. (Shikishima no Yamato-gokoro wo hito towaba, Asahi ni niou Yamazakura-bana: The Japanese spirit is like mountain cherry blossoms, radiant in the morning sun.)

By the morning of 20th October the kamikaze corps had been born, and Admiral Ohnishi who had stayed overnight at Mabalacat addressed the first twenty-four potential suicides after breakfast that day 'Japan is in great danger,' he said. 'The salvation of our country is now beyond the power of the ministers of state, the General Staff, and lowly commanders like myself. It can come only from spirited young men such as you. Thus, on behalf of your hundred million countrymen, I ask of you this sacrifice and pray for your success.' Then, in a voice shaking with emotion, he concluded: 'You are already gods, without earthly desires. But one thing you want to know is that your own crash-dive is not in vain. Regrettably we will not be able to tell you the results. But I shall watch your efforts to the end and report your deeds to the Throne. You may all rest assured on this point . . . I ask you all to do your best.' The effect of this speech on the doomed volunteers is not recorded. But Ohnishi returned to Manila, apparently very pleased with his creation. 'The fliers are eager and have formed a good unit . . .', he reported to Admiral Teraoka at Toyota's supreme headquarters later that day.

20th October 1944 was a memorable day for the suicide corps. While Ohnishi was scurrying back to Manila to report the successful inauguration of the Shimpu unit, steps were already being taken to form a second group of Kamikazes. Commander Nakajima, who had returned to Mabalacat from Manila early that morning, was ordered to fly to Cebu, 400 miles south of Manila, with the Yamato section and raise a second 'special attack' unit. With an escort of three other fighters, the five Zeros of the Yamato section touched down at the Japanese naval air base a few miles north of Cebu in the late afternoon. The purpose of Nakajima's mission had not been revealed, and even the pilots of the escorting fighters were unaware that their colleagues in the other Zeros had enrolled as kamikazes. But the unannounced arrival of eight Zeros at Cebu was something of an event. And when Nakajima promptly ordered a parade of all the flying personnel at the base, everyone there knew that he was there on some unorthodox assignment.

From a soap box on the edge of the strip, Nakajima addressed the assembled airmen. A review of the war situation was followed by an explanation of the purpose and importance of operation Sho. Finally the reason for his mission to Cebu was revealed:

'. . . The moment calls for the employment of crash-dive tactics. Admiral Ohnishi authorized such tactics last night at Mabalacat with the organisation of the Shimpu Special Attack Corps. Four units – Shikishima, Yamato, Asahi and Yamazakura – of this corps were activated at Mabalacat. Four of the planes that have just arrived with me consistute the Yamato unit . . .

'I have come to Cebu to organise another special attack unit. Any non-commissioned officer or enlisted flier who wishes to volunteer should submit his name to me by 2100 today.

'Everybody is not expected to volunteer. We know you are all willing to die for Japan . . . we also realize that some of you feel that family ties will preclude you from offering your life in this way. Furthermore the number of volunteers who can be accepted is limited by the availability of planes. As you all know we have only a very few aircraft . . . Only I will know whether a man volunteers or not, and because secrecy is vital to the operation there must be no discussion among yourselves. But special attack operations are expected to start

tomorrow, and that is why I want everyone of you to think things over and come to a decision before 2100 . . .'

The fliers had listened in complete silence, and when Nakajima stepped down from his box and the order was given to dismiss, they moved away quietly. But no mention had been made of officer volunteers in the speech, and soon after he had arrived at the officers' mess, Nakajima was accosted by two officers. The first, Lieutenant Yoshiyasu Kuno, was the pilot of one of the escort Zeros which had flown from Cebu. Kuno had been asleep when the arrangements of the first group of volunteers had been completed at Mabalacat, and he came to offer his services. The second, a bellicose young ensign of the Cebu squadron, claimed to represent the officers of the Cebu base. Officers had not been invited to volunteer, he said. Yet he and his colleagues were all eager to do so.

Shortly after 9pm an orderly brought Nakajima a pile of envelopes. Eighteen of them contained the formal agreement to volunteer for kamikaze duty for which he had asked at the parade. A second *Shimbu* unit was now assured.

Meanwhile, another sort of kamikze was being developed in Japan. During the summer months a certain Ensign Ohta had also been thinking about suicidal crash-dive tactics while flying cargo to Rabaul. To Ohta it was already clear that unless some radical new method of stopping the seemingly irresistible American advance was found quickly, Japan itself would be invaded. His ideas crystallised in a piloted bomb which could be carried into action by a Type-1 Betty bomber. Tokyo University was asked to help with the design, and plans had been drafted by the university's aviation research department by the end of September (1944). Sceptical at first, the Naval High Command, began to see possibilities in the weapon about the same time as Ohnishi was campaigning for kamikazes. In conse-

quence the first of the piloted glide bombs came off the production line towards the end of October, while other more complex versions of it were being developed.

The first of these weapons was not actually used until March 1945, and by then it was too late to swing the tide of battle. But a 'Special Attack Unit' was formed at the Koh-no-Ike airbase north-east of Tokyo to train pilots for the new weapon. (Subsequently, in April 1945 the special attack unit, commanded by a do-or-die enthusiast by the name of Captain Motoharu Okamura, was transferred to Kanoya.) Like the more 'conventional' Kamikaze pilots the young men who flew the weapon were all volunteers. Most of them were youngsters who had only the minimal training necessary for their mission. But as the war closed in on Japan they were joined by a few hard-bitten veterans from the remnants of the Japanese air force.

The first of Ohta's weapons, the *Okha* were tiny single-seater aircraft with rocket motors which had 2,640 pounds of explosive packed into the nose. As aeroplanes their performance was strictly limited and the mother aircraft had to launch them within ten miles of their target. From an altitude of 20,000 feet an *Okha* had a range of about fifteen miles and the pilots were taught to correct their glide path with short blasts of the rocket motors. The system was comparatively simple: en route to the combat zone the *Okha* pilot travelled in the mother bomber. Approaching the target area he would climb through the bomb-bay into his bomb, and when the pilot of the bomber had confirmed the target and aligned his plane the *Okha* would be released. When this happened there was no return, and it was a one-way ride for the *Okha* pilot.

'All for the Emperor, we are happy to die for him'; a message on the flag to be carried by one of the pilots on his suicide mission

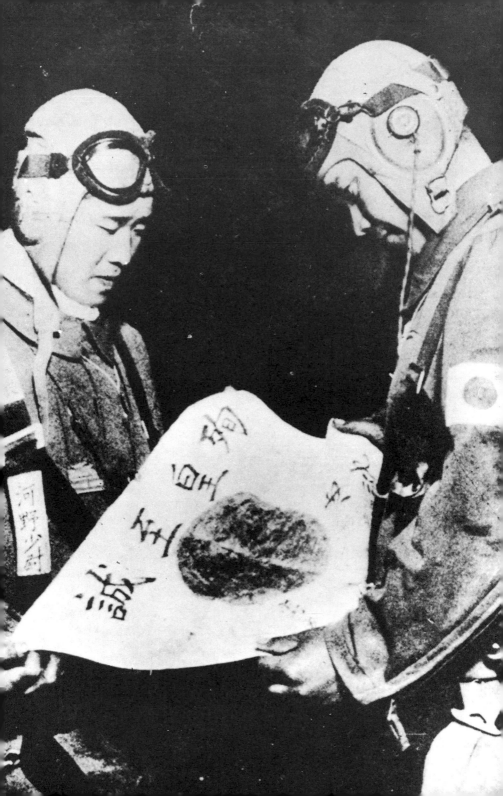

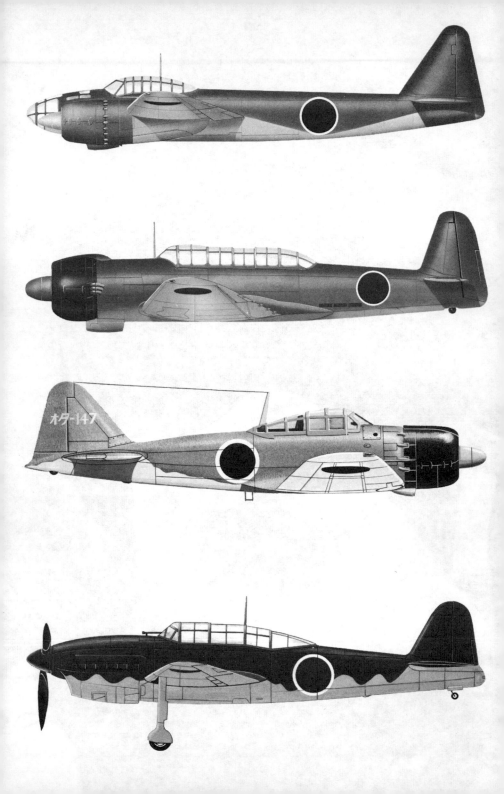

The Yokosuka P1Y1 Ginga (Milky Way), codenamed FRANCES by the Allies, was the Japanese Navy's standard fast medium bomber at the end of the war. Fast and manoeuvrable, the Ginga proved popular with pilots, but its troublesome hydraulic system and unreliable engines made it a mechanic's nightmare. *Engines:* two Nakajima NK9B Homare 11 radials, 1,820hp each at take off. *Armament:* up to 2,205 pounds of bombs or one 1,764 pound torpedo plus two 20mm Type 99 cannon. *Speed:* 340mph at 19,335 feet. *Climb:* 4 minutes 15 seconds to 9,845 feet. *Ceiling:* 30,840 feet. *Range:* 2,900 miles maximum. *Weight empty/loaded:* 16,017/29,762 pounds. *Span:* 65 feet 7$\frac{3}{32}$ inches. *Length:* 49 feet 2$\frac{9}{16}$ inches

The Nakajima B6N2 Tenzan (Heavenly Mountain), codenamed JILL by the Allies, was a single-engined three-seat carrier-borne torpedo bomber, but was used from land bases when the Imperial Japanese Navy's carriers were for the most part sunk or out of action towards the end of the war. The Tenzan was used very aggressively in both conventional and suicide roles in the Okinawa campaign. *Engine:* one Mitsubishi MK4T Kasei 25 radial, 1,850hp at take off. *Armament:* 1,764 pounds of bombs or one torpedo, plus two 7.7mm Type 97 machine guns. *Speed:* 299mph at 16,075 feet. *Climb:* 10 minutes 24 seconds to 16,405 feet. *Ceiling:* 29,660 feet. *Range:* 1,644 miles maximum. *Weight empty/loaded:* 6,636/12,456 pounds. *Span:* 48 feet 10$\frac{3}{8}$ inches. *Length:* 35 feet 7$\frac{3}{4}$ inches

The Mitsubishi A6M Reisen (Zero Fighter), codenamed ZEKE by the Allies, was the Japanese Navy's standard fighter throughout the Second World War, despite its obsolescence after the end of 1943. Like many other types not designed for the task, the Reisen was used as a suicide type in the closing stages of the war. For this purpose it was fitted with a 551 pound bomb. Specification for the standard A6M5 fighter illustrated. *Engine:* one Nakajima NK1F Sakae 21 radial, 1,130hp at take-off. *Armament:* two 20mm Type 99 cannon and two 7.7mm Type 97 machine guns. *Speed:* 351mph at 19,685 feet. *Climb:* 7 minutes to 19,685 feet. *Ceiling:* 38,520 feet. *Range:* 1,194 miles maximum. *Weight empty/loaded:* 4,136/6,065 pounds. *Span:* 36 feet 1$\frac{1}{16}$ inches. *Length:* 29 feet 11$\frac{3}{32}$ inches

The Yokosuka D4Y Suisei (Comet), codenamed JUDY by the Allies, was designed as dive bomber, but weaknesses in its wing spars meant that the type was at first used in the reconnaissance role. Improvements in the strength of the wing enabled the navy to accept the Suisei as a dive bomber in March 1943. The type was first used in suicide attacks during the battle for the Philippines, in the D4Y2 form illustrated here. Towards the end of 1944, the design was specially modified for the kamikaze role as the D4Y4. In this model, the position for the radio operator/gunner was done away with, a 1,764 pound bomb was let into the belly of the aircraft and three Rocket Assisted Take-Off Gear units were attached to the fuselage, either to shorten take-off run from short airstrips or to boost the Suisei's final diving speed onto the target. 296 of this type were built. *Engine:* one Aichi AE1P Atsuta 32 inline, 1,400hp at take-off. *Armament:* 1,234 pounds of bombs normally, plus two 7.7mm Type 97 machine guns and one 7.92mm Type 1 machine gun. *Speed:* 360mph at 17,225 feet. *Climb:* 4 minutes 36 seconds to 9,845 feet. *Ceiling:* 35,105 feet. *Range:* 2,239 miles maximum. *Weight empty/loaded:* 5,809/10,192 pounds. *Span:* 37 feet 8$\frac{3}{4}$ inches. *Length:* 33 feet 6$\frac{3}{4}$ inches

Kamikaze
in the
Philippines

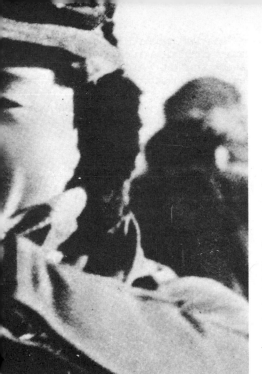

On 25th October, at 7.25am, nine planes rose from Mabalacat and headed east over the vast and lonely Pacific. Five of the planes were suicide craft – the *Shikishima* unit of the newly formed Special Attack Corps; the other four were escorts. Lieutenant Seki commanded the formation. Seki had been the first officer volunteer, and he was to draw the first blood in the new wave of suicidal strikes. All five pilots were hoping to die for their Emperor, and all wore the traditional *hachimaki* around their foreheads. For four consecutive days prior to the 25th they had worn the *hachimaki*, and taken off expecting their next mission would be from Yasukuni. On each occasion they had returned to their base frustrated if not actually disappointed. An American task force was known to be operating west of the Philippines, but whenever a suicide sortie was made the US ships evaded location. One reason for this was the lack of reconnaissance due to the loss of reconnaissance aircraft

in the American raids on the Philippine airfields. But the weather was also to blame. Without radar the Japanese were rarely able to locate American ships in the rain squalls which frequently descended on the area at this time of the year. Seki, who was determined to be the first successful kamikaze, was said to have expressed bitter disappointment when he returned from these abortive sorties. And Lieutenant Kuno, who was equally determined to be the first Special Attack pilot to die, announced his intention of flying off on his own to Leyte Gulf if no US ships were sighted on his official mission. At Leyte, he said, 'there were sure to be many targets'. In the event, what happened to Kuno will never be known. He failed to return on 21st October, but as no American ships were sunk or damaged by suicide attacks that day it is presumed he ran out of fuel somewhere over the Pacific.

Seki's planes reached Leyte Gulf about 10.40am, and on this occasion there was no rain squall to obscure the unsuspecting US warships. Seki had arrived at the perfect psychological moment. For hours the American fleet had been running before the brute power of Admiral Kurita's force, which had burst out of the San Bernardino Straits and turned south to destroy the fleet off Leyte. The carriers and destroyers had fought a tremendous delaying action against Kurita. It was only within the hour that the Japanese had turned and gone back, fearing a trap by other American units somewhere in the general area.

On board the *St Lo* and her sister carriers the crews were relaxing after their close rendezvous with extinction. Thus when Seki sighted them, the Americans had their guard down. The Japanese flew in low. At 1050, a warning went out to the carriers: 'Enemy aircraft coming in fast from

Admiral Takeo Kurita

'The *Shikishima* Unit of the Kamikaze Special Attack Corps made a successful surprise attack on an enemy task force containing four aircraft carriers at a point thirty miles northeast of Suluan Island at 1045 hours. Two planes hit one carrier, which was definitely sunk. A third plane hit another carrier setting it aflame. A fourth hit a cruiser which sank instantly.'

Elated by the first success of his new suicide corps, Ohnishi ordered the aerial attacks to be pressed home. It was now the turn of the *Yamato* section, and on the morning of 26th October eight Zeros took off from Cebu. They left in two groups; the first, of two kamikazes and one escort, departing at 1015, and the second, of three kamikazes and two escorts at 1230. As only one of the escorts of the second group survived, there is no record of which plane struck which target. But it appears that the kamikazes caught the American ships off guard in Leyte Gulf, just as Seki had done the previous day. The US carriers were in the midst of recovering planes which had been just returning from an attack on Admiral Kurita's fleet. Some of these aircraft were landing, some were on deck being refuelled and rearmed, and some were in the process of being launched when the suicide squadron discovered them. Without further ado the first Japanese pilot put his Zero into a dive on the escort carrier *Santee*. Machine guns blazing, he swept down on his target, crashed into the flight deck and penetrated to the hangar deck before his bomb exploded. A fire started but was quickly brought under control. Forty-three men were injured, however, a third of them fatally, and a huge hole was smashed in the forward deck. (A few minutes later the submarine I-56, one of several Japanese undersea craft operating in the area, put a torpedo into *Santee*'s starboard side. This might have been fatal, but *Santee* was sturdily built and survived the torpedo and continued in action.) Barely

overlying haze:' At 1053, a plane roared in over the *St Lo*'s ramp, then went into a steep dive and crashed on the flight deck near the centre line. At 1056, the gas below decks ignited. Two minutes later a violent explosion rocked the ship. A huge section of the flight deck was gone. Flames roared up 1,000 feet. By 1100 the *St Lo* was a mass of flames and she sank twenty-one minutes later.

While the *St Lo* burned, the other suicide planes banked and screamed straight into their targets. Not one missed. The *Kitkun Bay*, the *Kalinin Bay* and the *White Plains* were torn by explosions as steel smashed into steel at hundreds of miles per hour. Five planes had hit four ships. One carrier was sunk, the others badly damaged. Seki's success dispelled the one fear that had existed in the minds of those responsible for directing the kamikaze attacks – that when a plane dived the pilot might instinctively close his eyes before crashing and so miss his objective.

That night Tokyo radio broadcast a momentous communique from Imperial Headquarters:

Above: Aircraft of Lieutenant Seki's formation dives on the *USS White Plains*
Below: The *USS St Lo* blows up after a direct kamikaze hit

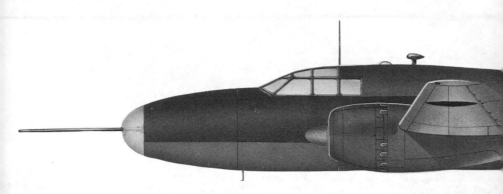

The Mitsubishi Ki-67-I KAI was the suicide version of the Japanese Army Air Force's best bomber, the Ki-67 Hiryu (Flying Dragon), codenamed PEGGY by the Allies. The modifications to turn a Ki-67-I into a I Kai were undertaken by the Tachikawa Dai-Ichi Rikugun Kokusho, and consisted of removing all the turrets and fairing over the holes thus made, reducing the crew positions from eight to three and installing the explosive charge (two 1,764 pound bombs or an explosive charge of 6,383 pounds) and the long rod projecting from the nose which detonated the explosives on impact with the target. Specifications for standard bomber Ki-67. *Engines:* two Army Type 4 (Mitsubishi Ha-104) radials, 1,810hp each at 7,220 feet. *Armament:* 1,794 pounds of bombs plus one 20mm Ho-5 cannon and four 12.7mm Type 1 machine guns. *Speed:* 334mph at 19,980 feet. *Climb:* 14 minutes 30 seconds to 19,685 feet. *Ceiling:* 31,070 feet. *Range:* 2,360 miles maximum. *Weight empty/loaded:* 19,068/30,347 pounds. *Span:* 73 feet $9\frac{3}{16}$ inches. *Length:* 61 feet $4\frac{7}{32}$ inches

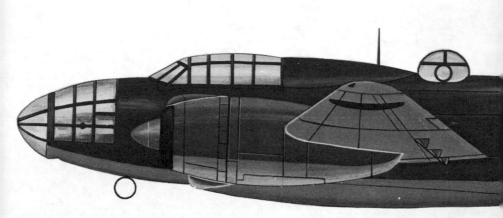

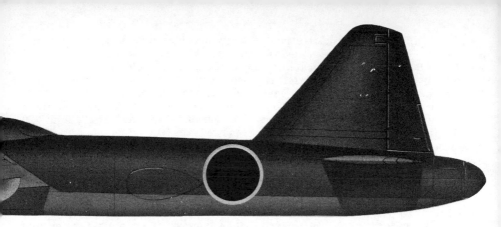

The Mitsubishi G4M, codenamed BETTY by the Allies, was the Japanese Navy's most famous bomber of the Second World War, and served right throughout the period of hostilities. After considerable initial successes where fighter opposition was negligable, the G4M suffered very heavy casualties as the Allies recovered from their first setbacks and started to bolster their aerial defences with more modern aircraft. The type's main failings were its lack of armour protection for the crew members and the fact that the fuel tanks were unprotected. Later on, these shortcomings were improved upon, but the type was always very prone to battle damage. At the end of the war, several models were adapted to carry the Okha suicide bomber, but the combination was so slow and heavy that it was an easy prey for Allied fighters. *Engines:* two Mitsubishi MK4T-B Ru Kasei 25b Ru radials, 1,825hp each at take off. *Armament:* 2,205 pounds of bombs or one torpedo plus four 20mm Type 99 cannon and two 7.7mm Type 92 machine guns. *Speed:* 292mph at 16,895 feet. *Climb:* 20 minutes 10 seconds to 22,965 feet. *Ceiling:* 30,250 feet. *Range:* 2,694 miles. *Weight empty/loaded:* 18,409/27,558 pounds. *Span:* 82 feet 0$\frac{1}{4}$ inch. *Length:* 63 feet 11$\frac{23}{32}$ inches

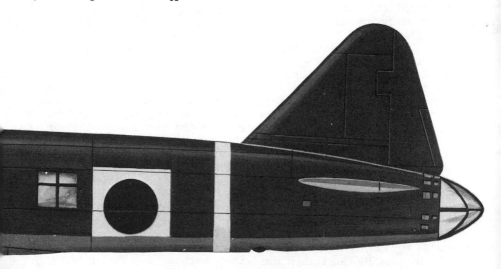

a moment after the kamikaze struck *Santee* the escort carriers *Suwanee* and *Petrol Bay* each downed an attacking suicide plane. Still another fell to *Suwanee*'s gunners before the last kamikaze hit and smoking plunged into the carrier and exploded between the flight and hangar decks. Damage was extensive and casualties numerous, although *Suwanee* was back in action in another two hours.

The cost of disabling the *Santee* was high. Seki's attacks, however, were considered to have been relatively successful. Indeed when compared with Japanese conventional air assaults, the kamikaze strikes of 25th October did remarkably well. According to plan, General Tominaga's Fourth Air Army planes were over the invasion beaches at Leyte in greater numbers that day, but could not do much damage. Scores of Japanese land-based naval planes were also out in strength searching for American warships. But either because of bad weather or lack of skill on the part of the inexperienced pilots, they were unable to find their targets. Thus, as two survivors of the kamikaze corps later put it: 'The superiority of special attacks was manifest . . . Hundreds of planes making orthodox attacks could not inflict as much damage on the enemy as a mere handful of kamikazes.'

Admiral Ohnishi had never been in doubt about the success of his suicide venture. A message from the Emperor praising the 'magnificent efforts of the *Shikishima* units', queried whether it was 'necessary to go to this extreme . . . ?' In Hirohito's language this was tantamount to a rebuke. Ohnishi was upset by it but undeterred, and when the Japanese high command in the Philippines conferred on 26th October, he pressed for an extension of the Special Corps' organisation. Those who had been reluctant to support Ohnishi's original proposals for suicide squadrons now began to revise their ideas. By this time it was patently clear that the Imperial

Navy had just suffered a catastrophic defeat. Whatever success had attended Operation *Sho* could be attributed to the unorthodox tactics which Ohnishi had initiated. Admiral Fukudome, commander of the Japanese Second Air Fleet based on Clark Field had opposed the introduction of suicide attacks. Indeed, he still favoured conventional mass-formation bombing and was uneasy about the possible effects on morale if his pilots were to be ordered to become kamikazes. But he could not deny the evidence of the effectiveness of Onishi's tactics and so, reluctantly, he agreed to an amalgamation of the two air fleets in which the main offensive element would be kamikaze units.

The 'Combined Land-Based Air Force', under the command of Admiral Fukudome with Ohnishi as his chief of staff, came into being on the evening of 26th October. There was no shortage of volunteers for the new strike force, and within twenty-four hours seven new Special Attack units had been formed. And as they were thrown into battle more volunteers came forward to take their place. Thus the limitation was not men but machines. As anticipated the results of the attacks went far beyond those possible by orthodox methods. To begin with the main kamikaze weapon was the Zero, but as time passed Val and Judy dive bombers and Frances twin-engined bombers were added to the kamikaze armoury. Stimulated by Ohnishi's successes the Japanese Army's air force units in the Philippines asked if they also might participate in the new offensive. Soon the Navy groups were joined by Army pilots and air crews in the increasing suicide bomb attacks. Yet, despite the high rates of strikes against the US warships and transports the Japanese could not stop the American invasion. The initial US carrier-borne attacks on the Japanese airfields in the Philippines had accomplished their purpose; in consequence Fukudome and Ohnishi just did not have

enough aircraft to thwart the American operations.

During October 1944 a typical kamikaze sortie was usually composed of three suicide planes with two escorts. The idea was to keep the attack formation small and a flight of five was considered the optimum number – big enough to ensure the annihilation of a single capital ship, yet small enough to evade interception and keep together in cloud and bad weather. The ratio of three kamikazes to two escorts was not a rigid one. But escorts were considered to be essential, to ward off American fighters while the kamikazes completed their fateful dives. To do so they had to stay at the side of the kamikazes and shield the suicide planes even if it meant their own sacrifice. Because the escort duty demanded superior flying skill and ability the best pilots were appointed as escort fliers, and their requests to volunteer for suicide missions were invariably turned down.

Damage was extensive and casualties numerous; *USS Suwanee's* hangar deck after a suicide attack

Admiral Kurita's defeat in the battle of Leyte Gulf was more than the failure of Operation *Sho*. Losses amounting to 3 battleships, 4 aircraft carriers, 9 cruisers, 13 destroyers and 5 submarines spelled the death warrant of the Imperial Japanese Navy. Officers and men aboard the remaining ships were still reported to be 'full of fighting spirit'. But more than fighting spirit was needed at this stage. For this reason it was decided to extend the operations of the Special Attack Corps, and Ohnishi's kamikazes were given a new objective. The naval planes would cooperate with the army in an attempt to smash the US beach head on Leyte. And to stop the Americans reinforcing the troops that had already been landed, the kamikazes would now attack troop transports as well as aircraft carriers.

By early November, however, the

'Combined Land Based Air Force' had exhausted most of its planes in suicide operations, and the trickle of reinforcements from Japan could not match the heavy losses. With Fukudome's approval, Ohnishi flew back to Japan to demand 300 planes specially for kamikaze operations in the Philippines. Imperial Headquarters in Tokyo, aware of the critical situation at Leyte, was willing enough to give Ohnishi all the aircraft he wanted. The trouble was that 300 planes were just not available. Only by depleting the training centres at Ohmura, Genzan, Tsukuba and Koh-no-Ike was it possible to muster even 150. And these planes would have to be flown by instructors and young pilots, few of whom had had more than a hundred hours flying training. It was a disappointing response, but Ohnishi was happy to grab what he could get. The planes were promptly organised with a new Special Attack Corps and transferred to Formosa for a week's training before being transferred to the Philippines.

In a week little could be done to improve the standard of training of the young pilots who suddenly found themselves committed to a suicide role. There was time only for the essentials. So two days were spent practising take-offs, two days to formation flying, and the last three days were given over to study and practice of the tactics that the kamikazes would employ in their attacks. Experience in the operations over Leyte Gulf had shown that certain methods of attack were more certain of success than others, and the new recruits concentrated on the newly accepted procedures.

Two methods of attack had been approved for the fast and manoeuvrable Zero fighter, and the 'Judy' bomber. The planes would approach their target flying either very high or at ground level. Both approaches restricted navigational accuracy and visibility, but more planes had got through to their targets this way than had the ones which flew in at a medium altitude.

At 18,000 to 20,000 feet it was completely easy to evade American fighters. Their presence could be expected to show up on the American's radar screens, of course. But it took time for the US fighters to climb to that altitude and they could be seen coming. Thus, the rule was the higher the altitude the greater the difficulty of interception.

The advantage of the alternative low-level approach accrued from the inability of US radar to detect the kamikazes until they were something less than ten miles from their target. Visual detection of aircraft skimming the wave tops was also difficult for American fighters screening their ships by routine patrols. At low level therefore the chance of interception was reduced to the minimum. When more than one attack unit was available, the ideal solution was to combine high and low level approaches in simultaneous convergent attacks, but the opportunities for doing this had been limited by the planes available.

For the final phase of their attack kamikaze pilots were taught not to make too steep a dive. Attacks made from a high altitude demanded a long, shallow controlled dive, and those making a low-altitude approach were told to climb to 1,000 feet when they spotted their target. This would enable them to start their dive about five miles away, giving a 45 degree angle of attack. Provided the kamikaze actually hit the target a near perpendicular dive was believed likely to be more effective. The trouble was that in a steep dive as speed increased control of the aircraft became progressively more difficult. Moreover the target would undoubtedly be frantically trying to evade the approaching hazard.

Other factors which had to be considered during the brief training session on Formosa were the point of aim – whereabouts the kamikaze should try to strike his target – and

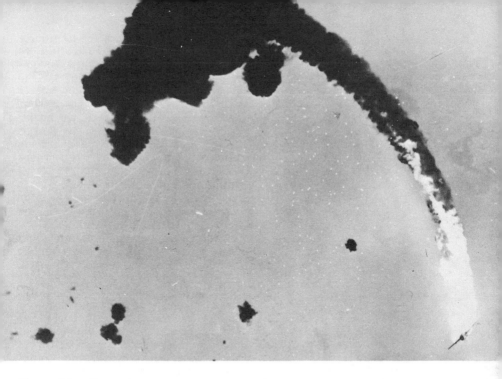

Above: A kamikaze plane, though on fire, attempts to crash *USS Wasp. Below:* Low-level attacks frustrate US radar

what tactics to adopt if the kamikaze formation were attacked during its flight to the combat area. Navigational training was also of extreme concern and most of the new pilots had only rudimentary grasp of what navigation really meant. In the normal course of events one trained pilot in an escort Zero could shepherd his suicides right up to the point where they headed for Yasukuni. But on numerous occasions kamikaze flights lost their leader in bad weather, or were separated from him in a dog fight.

Nervous excitement and emotional tension are factors which can be overcome only by repetitive drill. And there was no time on Formosa to reduce every action to a perfect drill. In consequence there were occasions when kamikazes were reported as having been seen to achieve direct hits on their targets, but failing in their missions because the bombs they carried did not explode. The simple explanation was that the pilots concerned had failed to arm their bombs before making the final plunge. This meant the loss of pilot and plane usually for an unprofitable return. In concentrating on making sure that he did hit the target in a vulnerable spot the pilot had omitted a vital step in the process of his self-immolation. It was possible of course to instruct the fliers to arm their bombs as soon as they took off, and were clear of the base airfields. But if they were unable to find their targets or their missions were aborted for some other reason, the bombs would have to be jettisoned before they could land safely. The solution, ultimately, was to order the bomb safety to be released as soon as the targets were sighted and as they flew in, the flight commander would try to check that this had been done. Even so there were still some pilots who forgot.

A high-level attack; this evaded US fighters

Above: A Japanese 'Frances' kamikaze aircraft about to crash after missing *USS Ommaney Bay*. *Below: USS Intrepid* is less lucky: a suicide airplane strikes

**A damaged dive bomber plunges into
*USS Kitkun Bay***

The 150 planes and the embryo kamikazes were collected and despatched to Formosa surprisingly quickly. (Surprising because most things in Japan were in a chaotic state by this time.) Even more surprising most of the planes and pilots actually arrived. With skilled pilots and aircraft in good condition, a thirty per cent casualty rate was accepted en route, when reinforcements were sent to the Philippines, so the loss of only ten aircraft during the concentration at Formosa may be regarded as something of a miracle. In the event the seven day training programme was completed by the middle of December and the new corps was rushed to the Philippines.

It arrived shortly after the Americans had landed on Mindoro Island. By this time also Fukudome and Ohnishi had moved their headquarters out of Manila to Clark Field, and were preparing for the imminent battle which would decide possession of Luzon. As the planes arrived kamikaze sorties were mounted, and the US ships in Leyte were constantly under attack until Fukudome ordered the shattered remnants of his two Air Fleets to withdraw to Formosa. By this time the entire Japanese air strength in the Philippines had been reduced to fewer than a hundred planes, and more than half of the new kamikazes had flown to their doom.

As the Americans consolidated their grip on Leyte and prepared for an assault landing on Luzon, they bombed the Japanese installations in-

effort by every pilot under his command. By throwing every plane he had at the Americans he hoped to deter them sufficiently to postpone what was clearly an assault landing operation. Only forty serviceable aircraft could be mustered. And when these were bombed up, the ground crews were marched off to join the Japanese army, vainly attempting to stem the tide of US might by stubborn suicidal resistance.

During the morning of 5th January, fifteen bomb-laden kamikazes escorted by two Zeros took off from Mabalacat; eight kamikazes with the same number of escorts from Echague; and five unescorted kamikazes from Angelo. All were ordered to select targets from the convoys in Lingayen Gulf. Which particular kamikaze hit which particular ship will never be known. But seven US naval vessels in the Luzon area were damaged by suicide attacks that day. None was destroyed, although one or two of the escorting Zeros which survived the attacks and returned to base reported that some ships were sunk.

That afternoon, and again the following day, the diminishing number of planes which returned to the Japanese airfields were refuelled, rearmed, and re-dispatched on other suicide missions. In the end nothing remained; not even a single Zero escort. In the Philippines the kamikazes were finished. In less than three months they had made 424 sorties and used 249 planes – of which 238 were Zeros – as piloted bombs. In terms of men and materiel they had exacted a terrible toll from the Americans. Not so great as they believed at the time, but nonetheless formidable. Nothing like this had ever been known before, and although the Americans were not daunted, they were shocked by such savage sub-human tactics. They knew that their own ultimate objective was Tokyo, and by the way the Japanese resistance was mounting they could look forward to nothing less than a suicidal blood bath.

cessantly. In the course of these raids, some of the kamikazes based on Clark Field became casualties. The comment of one survivor of such a bombing is worth recording, if only to illustrate the attitude of the would-be suicides. 'We are lucky', he is reported to have said. 'Until we hit the enemy our lives are very dear. We can't afford to squander them by getting killed carelessly.' Morale, it seems, was not a problem among the kamikazes.

The last kamikaze attacks to be made in the Philippines were on 5th January, 1945, when a reconnaissance plane reported a group of 300 US vessels west of Mindoro Island and Ohnishi decided to attack them. When the same plane reported having sighted 700 other ships behind the first group, he called for the maximum

The first
kaiten strike

News that the Americans had seized Ulithi Atoll in the Carolines, where a deep water anchorage would provide an ideal fleet base, prompted the Japanese to launch their first *kaiten* attack. Twelve of the newly trained would-be suicides were selected for the strike. Among them was one of the two inventors of the weapon, Lieutenant Sekio Nishina. Determined to show the worth of his innovation Nishina was taking along a box containing the ashes of his deceased co-inventor. This would ensure that both would go to *Kudan* and be enshrined at Yasukuni together. A dedication ceremony was conducted at the Otsujima base during the afternoon of 7th November 1944. Vice-Admiral Shigeyoshi Miwa, commander of the Imperial Sixth Fleet, supervised the proceedings and explained the forthcoming operation to the *kaiten* pilots. Three fleet submarines, the *I-36*, *I-37*, and *I-47*, which were in the bay nearby, would transport four *kaiten* each to the vicinity of Ulithi where large numbers of

American ships were reported to be concentrating. The *kaiten* pilots were to sink the biggest ships they could find. A presentation of short swords and *hachimakis* followed, and that night there was a party for the twelve doomed men. Next morning they embarked and at 9am the *I-36* led the three *I*-class submarines out of the harbour. As they steamed slowly up the channel the crews on other ships lined the rails shouting 'banzai' and waving their caps in a farewell gesture.

The three submarines parted company not long after leaving port. *I-37* was to proceed towards Kossol Passage in the Palaus, to attack Allied shipping there. *I-36* and *I-47* meanwhile would head straight for Ulithi. Their mission was to attack the American invasion fleet at anchor, launching their *kaiten* through two different entrances to the atoll's giant lagoon. But *I-37* was fated not to reach her destination. Despite having six lookouts on the bridge whenever she surfaced she was spotted by the American destroyer *Nicholas* on 12th November. In a sudden and unexpected attack the *I-37* was caught before she could dive and take evasive action.

I-47 was under command of Lieutenant-Commander Zenji Orita, one of Japan's ace submarine captains. He steamed slowly for his destination, making twenty knots on the surface, until he came within range of the American patrol planes. He then submerged by day, surfacing at night to charge his ship's batteries and to pick up radio reports from Sixth Fleet headquarters at Kure. His ship and *I-36* were working in close cooperation with reconnaissance planes from Truk. They would provide reports on American shipping at Ulithi.

On 17th November the *I-47*'s radio picked up a message relayed by Tokyo reporting that one of the reconnaissance planes had seen a vast concentration of American ships at Ulithi

on the previous day. According to the pilot they appeared to be anchored in three groups, and he had seen battleships and carriers among them. Next day, fifty miles west of Ulithi, Captain Orita surfaced so that the *Kaiten* could be given a final check. All four were found to be in good working order. By noon on the 19th the submarine had closed to within a mile of the southern entrance of the Ulithi lagoon, and at midnight the four *kaiten* pilots began making their final preparations. Last minute messages were written and handed to Orita together with their wills; finally all four men wound their *hachimakis* round their heads.

Ensigns Akira Sato and Kozo Watanabe climbed into their *kaiten* at midnight while the submarine wallowed quietly on the surface. Lieutenants Nishina and Fukuda were able to defer their entry, because there were access tubes to their weapons from the submarine. (Access tubes to all *kaiten* were provided on later sorties, so that the submarine could remain submerged.) When the lids of their weapons had clanged shut, Orita dipped *I-47* beneath the waves and then edged the submarine stealthily forward to the very entrance of the lagoon. This manoeuvring occupied three hours, during which Sato and Watanabe sat in their *kaiten* – their only contact with the world outside being two telephone cables. At 3am Nishina and Fukuda struggled through the access tubes to their *kaiten*, Numbers One and Two. All was now set for the attack.

Four cables bound each *kaiten* to the submarine's deck during the voyage. Two of these had been loosened when the *I-47* surfaced at midnight; the other two could be released from inside the submarine. At 4am Captain Orita, guided by the twinkle of welding torches on the US ships which he

USS Mississinewa afire at Ulithi Atoll after the first suicide torpedo strike; she was the only casualty

could see in his periscope, declared that he was in the firing position. Over the telephone lines the four *kaiten* men reported they were ready for action.

'*Kaiten* Number One stand by, start your engine!' ordered Orita.

'Standing by', came Lieutenant Nishina's soft voice over the circuit.

The third cable on Number One *kaiten* was loosened. 'Start your engine!' said Orita.

Inside the submarine, a motor sound could be heard.

'Engine started'

'Ready?'

'Ready!'

'Go!'

The fourth cable was loosened. It was 4.15am, 20th November 1944. Captain Orita, peering through his periscope, could see just a trace of bubbling water for a moment, as Nishina's *kaiten* moved off. Final checks of position, depth and the course Nishima was to follow had been made. He was now on his run-in, under orders to penetrate as deep into the anchorage as he could before raising his periscope and selecting a target for attack.

Ensign Sato left at 4.20, followed by Watanabe and Fukuda at five minute intervals. The second and the third *kaiten* were to get inside, then move off to the right and left, respectively. Fukuda was to attack when just inside the lagoon. This, it was hoped, would throw the Americans into a panic, when ships began exploding at widely separated points. The last words heard from *kaiten* pilots in *I-47*'s conning tower were Fukunda's, '*Tenno heika banzai!*'. Long live the Emperor!

The four *kaiten* forged towards their targets at about thirty knots. Meantime the barely submerged *I-47*, suddenly freed of twelve tons of metal, had lurched towards the surface. Orita submerged again to periscope depth and headed south-east. He wanted to be well away from the mouth of the anchorage when the

99

US destroyers depth charge the
Japanese submarine I-36

kaiten completed their mission. He
also wanted a clear view of what
happened to take back to Japan. Thus
at 5am, the *I-47* surfaced again. It was
pre-dawn twilight and the crew was
edgy, for daylight comes quickly in
the South Pacific. The minutes ticked
past. Then, at 5.07, an orange flash
blossomed over Ulithi, and there was
a distinct boom from well within the
lagoon where Nishina was supposed
to hit a target.

At 5.11 another flash set the submarine's crew *banzai*-ing. The appearance of an American destroyer soon
stopped that, however. Orita dived,
but when the absence of depth charges
suggested the submarine had not been
spotted he surfaced again. The sun
was now up and the destroyer could
be seen threading its way through the
entrance to the Ulithi anchorage. At
5.52 the dull thud of another explosion
was reported by *I-47*'s sonar as coming

from the atoll. It seemed that at least
three of the *kaiten* had scored hits on
something.

Whether their missions were successful or not Orita concluded that all
four pilots were now dead, and at
6am he ordered a silent minute of
prayer for their souls. Then he dipped
his ship beneath the waters and
headed for home.

I-36 was not so lucky. Lieutenant-
Commander Teramoto, the captain,
shut Ensigns Taichi Imanishi and
Yoshihiko Kudo into their *kaiten*
from the deck shortly after midnight.
At 3am Lieutenants Kentaro Yoshimoto and Kazuihisa Touozumi climbed into their craft through the access
tubes. Everything seemed to be going
well until *I-36* reached the point
designated for launching. just off the
eastern entrance to the Ulithi lagoon.

There, at the very moment set for
firing, *kaiten* Numbers One and Two
were found to be stuck fast in their
racks. They could not be freed after
their engines had started. Then the

pilot of *kaiten* Number Four reported that his craft was leaking badly. The only weapon that could be despatched was Ensign Imanishi in Number Three, who was launched at 4.54am.

Yoshimoto and Toyozumi returned to the submarine through their access tubes, and the *I-36* surfaced briefly to take in Kudo. At this point the captain decided no more could be achieved, and when the *I-36* submerged he turned her bow towards the open sea. Shutting off all the motors the crew listened intently. At 5.45am an explosion was heard, and at 6.05 another. Soon afterwards a pattern of depth charges rocked the *I-36* and Teramoto decided it would be wise to get away from the area.

But the *I-36* was compelled to stay submerged while American destroyers overhead methodically searched the area for the submarine which they thought had fired conventional torpedos from the eastern entrance. Nineteen hours passed. By that time the air in the submarine was foul with fumes, and the crew was exhausted. No depth charges had been heard for more than an hour, and Teramoto decided that he would have to surface to get fresh air and charge his batteries. Shortly before midnight the tanks were blown and the vessel surfaced. It was dark night and as there was no sign of American ships Teramoto took a risk. Running north on the surface at maximum speed, he cleared the area without further incident.

I-36 and *I-47* both got back to Kure on 30th November. On 2nd December a special conference was held on board the *Tsukushi Maru*, flagship of the Sixth Fleet, to consider Orita and Teramoto's reports on the *kaiten* attacks. Over 200 staff officers and specialists attended, and there was a lot of discussion before the results were summarized by a staff officer of the Sixth Fleet. Men on board *I-47* had seen two fires, he said. And the crew of *I-36* had heard explosions. Photographs of Ulithi taken by a reconnaissance plane from Truk, on 23rd November, three days after the *kaiten* operation, were then produced. 'From these', declared the speaker, 'we can estimate that Lieutenant Nishina sunk an aircraft carrier, as did Lieutenant Fukuda and Ensign Imanishi. Ensigns Sato and Watanabe sank a battleship apiece!'

This was the conclusion the audience wanted to hear, and there was a great outburst of *banzais*. The Japanese high command had ordered *kaiten* to be produced in quantity, and news that the first strike had been an outstanding success was a great boost to the morale of the scores of young men in training. 'Die for the Emperor, but not in vain' was a good motto. Every embryo *Kaiten* pilot was positively looking forward to his death-dealing mission, when the news was circulated.

The Japanese estimate of ships destroyed was a complete fabrication. The only ship sunk in the operation was the US tanker *Mississinewa*.

More death
from the
skies

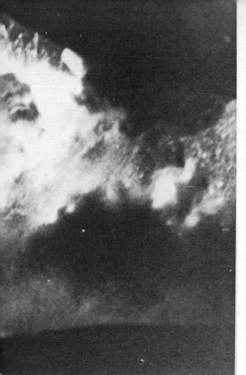

In November 1944, by a sheer stroke of luck, the Americans achieved an important success, of which they knew nothing until the war was over. About the same time as Ohnishi flew to Tokyo to press for reinforcements for his suicide squadrons, the first of the glide bomb pilots completed their training. According to the official records the *Jinrai Butai* (Corps of Divine Thunder) pilots were eager to show their mettle. So it was decided to give them their chance in the battle for the Philippines. In late November the giant 68,000-ton aircraft carrier *Shinano* left Yokosuka on its maiden voyage. In its hold were fifty of the new *Okha* bombs. On 29th November, the *Shinano* went to the bottom fifty miles south of Osaka, several hours after the US submarine *Archerfish* had put six torpedoes into the converted battleship. All fifty glide bombs were lost with the ship.

For two months no more of these weapons were available. The next batch was sent to Formosa, where Ohnishi's kamikazes were reorganised and regrouped. During the savage fight for Iwo Jima in February, Ohnishi sought an opportunity to throw some of the *Okha* bombs into battle. But it was not until 21st March that the *Okhas* were used in actual combat and in that time the 'conventional' kamikazes had been busy.

In Formosa Ohnishi set about reforming his old First Air Fleet from the training cadre which had supplied his reinforcements, and with the few trained kamikaze pilots who had escaped from the Philippines. The 'Combined Land Based Air Force' was no more and with it perished Fukudome's Second Air Fleet. In Japan also there was a frantic reorganisation to meet the next American thrust towards the homeland. Because the Imperial Navy had lost much of its surface strength in June 1944 in the Marianas, and most of the remainder in October at Leyte there was little chance of stopping the relentless American advance on Tokyo by naval action. Japan's only hope lay with what remained of her land-based air forces. By the end of the first week in February 1945 the air forces had been redeployed. But such pilots and crew as were available were sadly lacking in training and experience. Many of the pilots had not even completed their basic training, and it was obviously not going to be possible to have them ready for battle by April when the next American offensive was expected. In such circumstances orthodox aerial tactics had little chance of success, and Imperial General Headquarters now decreed that there was no alternative to the general use of suicide attacks. This was the only way in which inexperienced pilots could be expected to score a hit on the invasion fleets.

Ohnishi had interpreted the requirement in advance and his operational

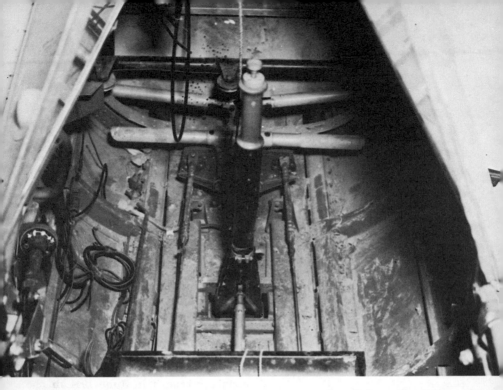

strength returns were already reflecting the wastage incurred by kamikaze attacks. On 18th January the first of his new special attack corps was formally dedicated at Tainan in north Formosa. This was the *Niitaka* Unit, so called after the Formosan mountain of that name. Ohnishi's speech to the young kamikaze pilots followed his usual line, emphasizing a soldier's duty to the Emperor and the Samurai principles. But on this occasion he made a point of adding, 'Even if we are defeated, the noble spirit of this kamikaze attack corps will keep the homeland from ruin. Without this spirit, ruin would certainly follow defeat.' The words 'even if we are defeated' presented a change of view. Up to this point Ohnishi had always maintained that the kamikaze tactics were necessary to ensure victory in war. Now, it seemed, there was a possibility of defeat, but the suicidal attacks were directed towards the more distant goal of perpetuating Japan in defeat.

Above: The controls in the cockpit of an Okha were simple but effective
Right: The Okha, a piloted bomb with no escape for the pilot after his release from a 'Betty' bomber

The first sortie made by the *Niitaka* Group took place on 21st January 1945. An American task force had been sighted south-east of Formosa and eleven *Niitaka* kamikazes flying in three separate sections were ordered to attack it. Each section was escorted by two Zeros, and the kamikazes flew other Zeros or 'Judy' bombers. As the airfield from which they were operating was constantly being raided by the Americans, there was some trepidation until the attackers were airborne. But they took off without mishap and apart from one section running into a patrol of US Grummans which promptly downed two of the kamikazes and dispersed the other aircraft of that particular section, their mission may be considered at least partially successful. The aircraft carrier *USS Ticonderoga*, the light carrier *USS Langley* and the destroyer *Maddox* were all damaged by suicide attacks that day.

Meanwhile, back in Japan naval technicians were working furiously to develop variations of the *Okha*. These included the jet propelled *Okha* Model 22, the turbo-jet propelled *Okha*, Model 33 and 43; the turbo-jet engined *Kikka* (Mandarine Orange Blossom); the pulse-jet *Baika* (Plum Blossom); and the *Shinryu* (Divine Dragon) glider which used solid rockets for the take-off. Not to be outdone by the Navy the Army also launched a programme to build the all steel *Tsurugi* (Sword), in which any type of internal combustion engine could be mounted. The naval version of this weapon was the *Toka* (Wisteria blossom). In the event, before the *Kikka*, *Shinryu* and *Tsurugi* had been test flown, the war had ended.

Even as the Imperial Navy and Japanese army laboured to perfect the new piloted bombs the kamikaze scene was shifting even closer to Japan. American aircraft were now regularly bombing targets in Tokyo, Yokohama and elsewhere on the Kanto plain. Kamikaze crash attacks were attempted in an effort to deter the huge B-29s, and aerial death struggles continued until the end of the war. Then came the invasion of Iwo Jima and it was decided to launch a massive suicide attack on the invasion fleet. This invasion was mounted by Admiral Kimpei Teraoka's Third Air Fleet, which was deployed at airfields in the Tokyo region. Early in the morning of 21st February 1945 thirty-two planes organised into five groups took off from Katori, refuelled at Hachijo Jima and then flew on to attack the great invasion fleet. That night Tokyo radio announced a US carrier and four transports sunk, while one other carrier and four other

Above: The forward flight deck of *USS Saratoga* after a kamikaze hit. *Below: USS Franklin* under suicide attack after US air raids on southern Japan

warships had been damaged. Subsequently the Americans confirmed that the carrier *USS Bismark Sea* had been sunk, and the carriers *Saratoga* and *Lunga Point*, together with a cargo ship and two landing ships, damaged off Iwo Jima on 21st February. Very few of the attacking planes returned to their bases from this operation. And it is noteworthy that the pilots of several of the escorting Zeros, ignoring orders, tried to ram their planes into the American fighters from which they were trying to protect the kamikazes, or to complete their mission by crashing into a US ship.

With the occupation of Iwo Jima in March, the over-all picture of the war was black indeed for Japan. The invasion fleet had disappeared south, clearly to prepare for another landing which would bring the Americans even closer to Tokyo. It was suspected to be harbouring, refuelling and refurbishing in the deep water at Ulithi Atoll in the Carolines. And on 9th March a reconnaissance *Salun* plane from Truk confirmed that this was so. The plan now was to try to cripple the invaders' fleet before another landing operation could be attempted, and its details had been worked out some time before. On 19th March the plan was put into effect. The attack was to be made by twenty-four *Ginga* (Frances) bombers. Each would carry a 2,000 lb bomb and be piloted by a kamikaze. Four flying boats would guide them to Ulithi, and the whole force would be preceded by a patrol of four other bombers.

Everything went according to plan and the *Azuyu* Special Attack Unit, as the twenty-four bombers were called took off. But before they had got half-way to their objective they were recalled. A photo-reconnaissance made by another plane from Truk had supposedly revealed that there was only one US carrier at Ulithi. By the time it was learned that this was a mistake – there were in fact eight US fleet carriers and seven escort carriers at Ulithi – it was too late to resume the operation that day.

But on the early morning of the 11th the planes took off again. The weather was bad and the kamikazes lost their guide planes in thick cloud. Thirteen of them also developed engine trouble en route and had to drop out. But the remaining eleven arrived undetected over the target area and dived on to the ships below. Not one returned to tell the tale. But in relation to the cost in men and effort the results were disappointing. Only the US carrier *Randolph* was hit and damaged in the raid.

By the beginning of March Japan's future looked ominous. Both the Army and Navy air forces were committed to kamikaze attacks, and the numbers of available aircraft were diminishing. *Shiragiku* navigational training aircraft, and various types of reconnaissance seaplanes, had been put to use to supplement the Zeros, Judies, Frances, Vals, Kates, Bettys, Nells and Jills that were now regarded as suicide mission planes.

On 19th and 20th March the Allied invasion of Okinawa was heralded by a series of massive US air attacks on targets in southern Japan. In response, about fifty kamikaze attacked the carriers which had brought the raiders and the USS *Essex, Franklin, Wasp* and *Enterprise* were all reported to have been damaged during the fierce air battles which took place on these days. The climax was yet to come, however. On the morning of 21st March a Japanese reconnaissance plane spotted three of these US carriers about 320 miles off Japan. All three appeared to have suffered damage, and, surprisingly no fighter cover was being maintained. There they were, wallowing in the water, completely unprotected.

When the report reached him, Vice-Admiral Matome Ugaki decided that this was the ideal opportunity to try out the *Okha*. Eighteen bombers began to load *Okha* weapons, and every available fighter in the whole of southern Japan was ordered up to

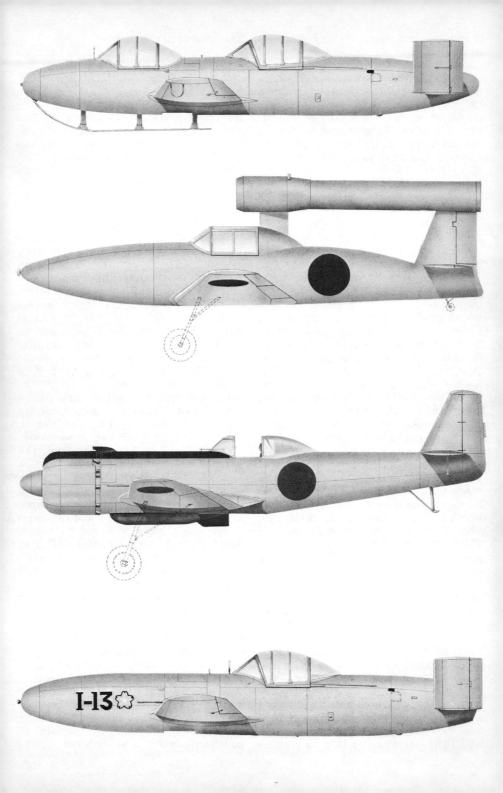

The Yokosuka Okha Model 43 K-1 KAI Wakazakura (Young Cherry) was a two-seat training version of the standard Okha suicide aircraft. The warhead was replaced by a second cockpit, and flaps and retractable skids were provided for landing. To enable the pupil to obtain some sort of handling the type with an engine, the Model 43 K-1 KAI was fitted with a Type 4 Mark 1 Model 20 rocket motor of 573 pounds thrust. Apart from this the Wakazakura was similar to the Model 11. Only two were built

Kawanishi Baika (Plum Blossom) was a projected piloted suicide aircraft which, inspired by the manned version of Germany's V-1, was still on the drawing boards when the Pacific War ended. The Baika was to have been fitted with a 550lb warhead and the pilot was intended to jettison his undercarriage after taking-off on his one-way mission. *Power Plant:* One Maru Ka-10 pulse jet of 795lb thrust. *Estimated maximum speed:* 460mph. *Weight loaded:* 3,150lb. *Span:* 21ft 7in. *Length:* 22ft 11in

Nakajima Ki-115 Tsurugi (Sabre) was specifically designed for the suicide mission and was the essence of simplicity. It could be powered by a variety of surplus engines, and a recessed crutch under the fuselage centre section could accommodate a single bomb of up to 1,764lb. The Tsurugi was designed and the first prototype built within two months, and 104 production examples had been rolled out by the time flight trials were completed in June 1945, although none was used operationally. *Power Plant:* One Nakajima Ha-35 14-cylinder radial of 1,130hp. *Maximum speed:* 340mph at 9,185ft. *Range:* 745 miles. *Weight empty:* 3,616lb. *Weight loaded:* 5,688lb normal, 6,349lb maximum. *Span:* 28ft 2½in. *Length:* 28ft 0½in

Yokosuka MXY7 Ohka (Cherry Blossom) suicide aircraft was conceived for coastal defence and as an anti-invasion measure. The Model 11 (illustrated) was intended to carry a 2,646lb warhead, and the first powered flight was made in November 1944, the first operational use of the weapon being made on 21st March 1945, the Ohka's first victims being the battleship *West Virginia* and three transport vessels which suffered heavy damage 11 days later. A total of 755 Ohka Model 11s was built, but only a small proportion of these saw action. *Power Plant:* Three Type 4 Mk 1 Model 20 solid-propellant rockets with total thrust of 1,765lb. *Maximum speed:* 402mph at 11,500ft. *Range:* 23 miles. *Weight empty:* 970lb. *Weight loaded:* 4,720lb. *Span:* 16ft 9in. *Length:* 22ft 6¾in

escort the bombers. Carrying the heavy *Okhas* the ponderous bombers would be slower than ever, and a powerful escort was necessary to make sure they got through to where the carriers had been sighted. But only fifty-five Zeros could be mustered, and because this was considered too few the operation was very nearly called off. According to the official report it was the enthusiastic determination and keenness of the *Okha* pilots which resulted in the decision to take the risk and let the operation proceed.

Commanding the bombers was a certain Lieutenant-Commander Goro Nonaka one of the few veterans who remained. He was said to be a hard man, 'who placed great emphasis on the traditional *samurai* spirit'. Nevertheless his unit was a happy one, and Nonaka was respected as an able leader.

Nonaka's senior was the forty-five-year-old Captain Okamura, who had grown grey in the service of the Imperial Navy's fleet air arm. It was he who had raised and organised the first *Okha* unit, and he was determined to vindicate his work by taking part in the very first *Okha* mission. When the aircraft were warming up Okamura announced that he was going to lead the attack. Nonaka was furious. He too was anxious to be the first *Okha* martyr, and apparently there was a somewhat unseemly argument on the airstrip before Okamura gave way.

Nonaka had obviously prepared his last speech and before climbing into the cockpit of his bomber he announced enigmatically 'This is Minatogawa.' The reference was to the shrine of that name at Kobe, which was erected to immortalize the 14th century patriot Masashige Kusunoki who said before his death '*Shichisei*

Another failure for the Okha. Gun-camera shots of a Japanese 'Betty' loaded with an Okha bomb, as it tries in vain to out-manoeuvre the attacking American fighter

hokuku!' – Would that I had seven lives to give for my country!

The eighteen bombers took off at 11.35am with Nonaka leading. All the pilots were wearing the customary *hachimaki* and as this was one of the biggest and most important operations for some time, the edge of the runway was lined with spectators from the base. Admiral Ugaki himself was there to see the kamikazes off, with tears in his eyes, it was said. Maybe his tears were for the brave men who would not return; possibly his thoughts were centred on the wretched depths to which his country had sunk. For the take-off was a depressing spectacle. Of the fifty-five Zeros assembled for escort duty, eight could not even get off the ground to follow the lumbering bombers, and seventeen others were forced to turn back along the way because of engine trouble. And no sooner were the planes airborne than a reconnaissance plane reported that the American carriers, surrounded by many more warships than was originally believed, had separated and the various groups were heading southwest.

With news like this the chances of the kamikazes' success were considerably reduced, and there was some argument on whether the operation should be called off before the planes got any further. While Ugaki hesitated, fifty Grumman fighters settled the issue. The escorting Zeros tried in vain to drive off the interceptors, who concentrated their efforts on the *Okha*-laden bombers. In consequence the bombers, powerless to fight back effectively, had to jettison their *Okhas* to lighten their load and increase their manoeuvrability. Even so, fourteen of them were shot down in quick succession, and nothing more was seen or heard of the four others after they dived into a cloud bank hotly pursued by Grummans.

So ended the first of the *Okha* sorties. Six months training brought suicide, but no return.

Above: *USS Enterprise* is attacked by a Japanese plane off southern Japan
Below: A suicide dive-bomb attack on USS Essex

Above: An Okha bomb, known to the Americans as a Baka, in a revetment in Japan
Below: US technicians study a Baka bomb captured on Okinawa

Samurai
under
the sea

Following the supposedly tremendous success of the first *kaiten* operation, a more ambitious offensive was planned. Six submarines, *I-36*, *I-47*, *I-48*, *I-53*, *I-56*, and *I-58*, carrying four *kaiten* apiece would strike American shipping concentrations simultaneously, at widely separated locations. After what had apparently been accomplished at Ulithi the Japanese high command felt that the sinking of twenty-four US capital ships, all about the same time, would have a devastating effect on the Americans' morale. This might induce a lull in their island chain offensive and provide an opportunity for Japan to catch her breath. There would then be time for the manufacture of more suicide weapons and the training of their operators and pilots.

The twenty-four pilots selected for the new series of strikes were designated the *Kongo* group. Each combat group was given a traditional title when its members finished their training. *Kongo* was the mountain near where the retainers of the old

feudal hero Magashiye Kusukoni had trained. Only fourteen of the group were launched, the remainder returned to 'final glory' with other *kaiten* groups formed for other operations at a later date.

The submarines sailed from Otsujima during the first week of January 1945. *I-36*, commanded by Lieutenant-Commander Teramoto returned to Ulithi Atoll for a second attack on the anchorage there. Orita's *I-47* which had also taken part in the first *kaiten* attack at Ulithi headed for the waters round New Guinea, where the campaign had been going badly for Japan. *I-48*, under Lieutenant-Commander Zenshin Toyama was supposed to back up the *I-36*, and she was believed to have been sunk off Ulithi on 22nd January. *I-53*, commanded by Lieutenant-Commander Seihachi Toyomasu, had been ordered to attack shipping lanes in the Palaus. *I-56*, under Lieutenant-Commander Masahiko Morinaga, was destined for the Admiralty Islands, west of New Britain, where the Americans and Australians were reported to have concentrated a large number of ships. Finally, *I-58*, under Lieutenant-Commander Mochitsura Hashimoto, made for Guam. Hashimoto became famous later. On 29th July 1945, while still in command of the *I-58*, he put three torpedoes into the US cruiser *Indianapolis*. After the war there was a rumour that this vessel was carrying an atomic bomb when she went down – intended to be the third nuclear weapon to be dropped on Japan. (This was denied by the Secretary for War, Mr Stimson, who said that the US had only two bombs. But in his memoirs President Truman says that there was a plan to drop a third bomb on Niigata.) Whether or not this was true, a serious view was taken of the loss of the *Indianapolis* and her captain was court-martialled. Hashimoto had the unusual experience of being a witness.

11th January was scheduled as the day on which the simultaneous attack should take place. Since the Kikusui operation much had happened. The Americans were winning in the Philippines, despite the fierce resistance offered by the Japanese army, and the damage inflicted by the kamikazes. American submarines, roaming freely in Japanese waters, were taking their toll of badly needed supplies to Japan. At the same time anti-submarine patrols were making it progressively more difficult for Japanese submarines to operate effectively. The *I-46* and *I-365* had been lost between November and January. The result was that nothing went according to plan. The submerged *I-36* ran on to an underwater shelf, from which she was dislodged with great difficulty. In the end her four *kaiten* were fired and the official appraisal was that four ships – including a battleship – had been sunk. Orita in the *I-47,* whose wardroom now contained a little shrine bearing the card 'My offering . . . one large aircraft carrier. Sekio Nishina', ' ran into trouble with an anti-submarine patrol. Nevertheless he got his *kaiten* away into Humboldt Bay, New Guinea. He too was credited with four kills, although the evidence to confirm any hits was largely circumstantial since he spent the next twenty-four hours dodging US destroyers. Nothing was heard of the *I-48* after 21st January. But she reported firing her four *kaiten* at targets in Ulithi – albeit two days late. She too was credited with four hits.

Undetected, Toyamasu's *I-53* managed to slip into a firing position off Kossol Passage in the Palaus, where there was a constrant stream of Allied shipping. Only three of his *kaiten* were fired, since the engine of one persistently refused to start. And of these three one mysteriously blew up just as it left the submarine. But the other two appeared to work all right, and their pilots, Ensign Ito and Petty Officer Arimori were each credited with a large transport.

In the Admiralties Commander Morinaga also made an undetected approach to his target area. Then *I-56* ran into trouble. The Allies had laid nets to form an anti-submarine barrier in front of their anchorage. Morinaga repeatedly tried to find a way through, but after getting stuck in the nets and only extricating the submarine with great difficulty he called off the operation and returned to Japan with all four *kaiten* intact.

Only Hashimoto's sortie may be said to have gone without a hitch. The *I-58* got to Guam safely, the four *kaiten* were fired, and their pilots, Lieutenant Ishikawa, Ensign Kudo and Petty Officers Mori and Mitsueda were credited with sinking an escort carrier and two large transports.

Sixth Fleet headquarters declared the whole operation had been a signal success, despite the loss of the *I-48.* *Kaiten* operations would be extended, and more pilots would be trained for the increasing numbers of the weapons now beginning to roll off the production lines. A new training centre was opened at Hikari and 200 new recruits for the suicide squad started to learn the rudiments of their one-way mission. By and large there were enough *kaiten* for the training programme. The bottleneck was a shortage of technicians to check and test the brand-new weapons. Training was also hampered by the need to conserve oil. During exercises in the bay each *kaiten* was mothered by a fast patrol boat. These boats used high-octane fuel which was becoming progressively more scarce. In consequence training in the advanced handling of a *kaiten* had to be cut to the bone.

When the Americans were seen to be preparing to invade Iwo Jima Combined Fleet Headquarters ordered the Sixth Fleet to attack the US task force with every available *kaiten*. For a submarine, Iwo Jima was a short run from Japan, a fact which would help to compensate for the shortage of *kaiten* launching platforms. The

Above: I-58 successfully launched four *kaitens* at Allied shipping off Guam
Below: A suicide torpedo ashore, ready for launching against invading ships

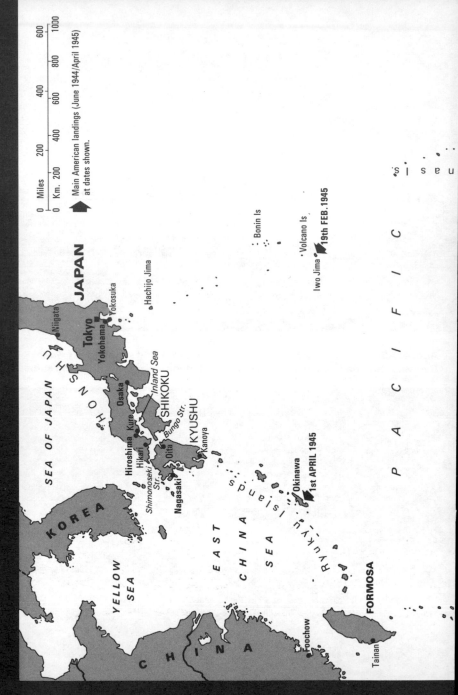

Japanese suicide attacks were used in an attempt to prevent the invasion of the Japanese home islands

submarines would not have to cruise so far to find a target. They would be able to return quickly, take on more *kaiten* and return to the battle in a very short time.

Ten *kaiten* pilots of the *Chihaya* Group left Otsujima and Hikari on 20th February 1945 in the *I-368* and *I-370*. The *Chihaya* Group was named after the castle south of Nara, Japan's ancient capital, which had been Kusunoki's home. None saw action as both submarines were sunk before they were able to do any damage. Three days later the *I-44* carrying another five *kaiten* men of the *Chihaya* Group also sailed for Iwo Jima. She returned on 9th March, with all *kaiten* intact. American anti-submarine patrols were so thick after the *I-368* and *I-370* were sunk, that the *I-44* could get nowhere near the target area. Every time her captain, Commander Genbei Kawaguchi, tried to

The largest Japanese submarines were almost twice the size of the United States' largest

surface to see what was happening, the presence of the *I 44* was detected. And after US planes and ships had kept her under the waters for nearly forty-eight hours, Kawaguchi called off the operation. When he got back to Otsujima Kawaguchi was promptly relieved of his command. The Imperial Navy had less patience than ever with officers who failed. Kawaguchi had thought it better to live and fight another day; his superiors did not agree with him.

I-58 and *I-36* sortied out with ten men of the *Shimbu* Group, 'God's Warriors', at the beginning of March. Like the I-44 they returned having accomplished nothing. On this occasion the captains retained their command; Sixth Fleet staff officers were beginning to appreciate that submarine operations against the Americans were no sinecure. The only way to break through, they decided, was by a mass attack. Every submarine which could carry *kaiten* would be fitted to take as many as possible. They would all sail together

to attack targets in the same area – off Okinawa. Here a kind of underwater *banzai* charge would be staged. Some *kaiten* would be certain to get through. The trouble was only four *kaiten*-carrying submarines were now available.

The operation was scheduled for the end of March, and the *Tatara* group (Tatara beach in northern Kyushu is where the Mongol armada was wrecked by the *kamikaze* typhoon) of *kaiten* pilots were embarked on the *I-44*, *I-47*, *I-56*, and *I-58*. Orita's *I-47* was designated the flagship for the *Tatara* Group's operation. Three of the submarines carried four *kaiten*, and the *I-56* had been refitted to take six. The objective of the attack was warships off Okinawa.

There was the usual party on the night of 26th March. A lot of *sake* was drunk, and Admiral Nagai, who had replaced Vice-Admiral Miwa as commander of the Sixth Fleet, wished the *kaiten* men 'every success'. 'I hope each of you will strike our enemy', he said. 'At that moment your souls will fly to Yasukuni, there to watch forever over God's country, Japan. Please be assured that the rest of us in Sixth Fleet will do everything possible to comfort those you leave behind . . .' Other senior officers made similar speeches exhorting the 'Samurai of the Sea' to 'do a good job'. Next morning, when they embarked, there were a few thick heads in the *Tatara* Group.

Like the previous operation with the *Shimbu* Group, the *Tatara* affair was an utter and complete failure. Even as the submarine pack approached the target area the Americans were storming ashore at Okinawa, and no less than 150 destroyers were screening the vast invasion fleet. Through this formidable barrier of anti-submarine patrols the Japanese submarines had little hope of penetrating. *I-44* and *I-56* were sunk in the attempt. *I-47* managed to escape and limp back to Japan, and *I-58* was chased off and compelled to withdraw. There were now not enough submarines to take out all the men who were being trained to handle *kaiten*, so by April most of them were scheduled to be employed in what was fancifully called 'base *kaiten* attack'. A plan was drawn up for *kaiten* to be deployed along Japan's coast, at points where an amphibious assault could most likely be expected. The *kaiten* pilots were expected to hide their weapons and wait. When the Americans were just off-shore, they would receive a signal from Imperial Headquarters. Then, the base *kaitens* would roar out to sea and sink as many troopships as possible. Japanese naval strategy had not changed – give the Americans a blood bath and smash them in one single decisive action. This was the strategy that had been used at Midway, the Marianas and the Philippines. Soon it would be used again at Okinawa. It had not yet worked to Japan's advantage but as the Americans closed in, and the suicidal patriotic fervour increased, hopes that it might do so remained high.

Suicidal climax

On Easter morning, 1st April 1945, American troops landed on Okinawa. This island was the next US objective in the final series of island hops to Japan. The Japanese expected it, and Tokyo radio had been talking about it for days. When the invasion came, a broadcast solemnly informed the people that 'It is a matter of a short time before the rise or fall of our people will be decided.' Okinawa, about 360 miles southwest of the major home island of Kyushu, was regarded as an integral part of Japan. Strategically

cliffs, and limestone and coral caves. On it the Japanese had constructed ingenious fortifications, interlocking and intercommunicating tunnels, concrete block houses, pill boxes and deep shelters. They were under no illusions – they had to defend this malaria-ridden island or lose the war. Okinawa was so important that they were prepared to risk everything to hold it. Two divisions and two brigades, commanded by Lieutenant-General Mitsura Ushijima, a naval force under Rear-Admiral Minoru Ota, and about 7,000 airmen commanded by a Captain Tanamachi – ground crews with no aircraft to service – were deployed in the fortifications. 70,000 men in all waited to repel the Americans.

Past experience had shown that the defenders would resist fiercely, and the Americans had planned the invasion with care. They had assembled the greatest invasion fleet ever to operate in the Pacific – 1,300 warships of all kinds and sizes – and there were 100,000 soldiers and Marines aboard them. This was the armada that the Japanese high command resolved to decimate.

That kamikaze air attacks and *kaiten* operations would be mounted against the invading force was a foregone conclusion. But when news reached Tokyo that the Americans had actually secured a bridgehead on Okinawa, Admiral Toyoda decided a greater effort was called for. As Commander-in-Chief of the once proud Combined Fleet, he decided that his remaining ships should make their contribution to the forthcoming *Götterdämmerung*.

After the Battle of Leyte Gulf which had seen the beginning of the Kamikaze Corps, the Imperial Navy had ceased to exist as a practical fighting force. Most of the cruisers had been lost, and the battleships *Yamato*, *Nagato* and *Haruna*, which had limped home, had been bottled up

it dominated the East China Sea and the Chinese coast from Foochow to Korea. It sat astride Japan's sea lanes to the oil-rich East indies, already endangered by the American occupation of the Philippines. Furthermore, from Okinawa B-29s could range over the Yellow Sea and Straits of Shimonoseki and return with fuel to spare.

Okinawa was built by nature for defence. Sixty-seven miles long and from three to twenty miles wide, its terrain was cut up in a maze of ridges.

in the Inland Sea. Shortage of fuel precluded their being used for operations. During March, however, an attempt had been made to resuscitate the Second Fleet, by allocating what remained of the dwindling fuel stocks to the *Yamato*, the cruiser *Yakagi* and five destroyers. It was this force that Toyoda proposed to use in a suicide assault on the US invasion fleet off Okinawa. There was little if any coordination between the services as to how the army, navy and air force would act and when. But for the first time in history a coordinated all-out suicide attack was to be launched – kamikazes cooperating with the submarines. A series of *kaiten* and kamikaze attacks had already been scheduled for 6th April under the code name *Kikusui*. Literally 'floating chrysanthemum', *Kikusui* was the crest of the Kusukoni family. In the 14th century Mazashige Kusukoni had led a Japanese army to certain death in a suicide operation. But *Kikusui* Operation No 1 was to be the grand attack which could make the other operations superfluous.

The warships of the reconstituted Second Fleet were commanded by Vice-Admiral Seeichi Ito, who had been Vice-Chief of Naval Operations in 1941, and who was considered to be an outstanding officer. Realising that desperate circumstances called for desperate action, Ito was willing to accept orders for a suicidal operation without questioning them. He was one of the few senior officers of the Imperial Navy who did. In Tokyo the Naval General Staff were against Toyoda's *Kikusui*, maintaining that although Japan faced total defeat it was inhuman to order men into an operation of this magnitude which was so uncertain of success. In their view the fleet would never reach Okinawa, so the loss of men and ships was a wasteful sacrifice. Toyoda's own Combined Fleet Headquarters refuted this argument. The loss of Okinawa would be disastrous, they said, and it was the navy's job to

cooperate with the army, The fleet might not reach Okinawa but it would attract the attention of a large number of American aircraft. A lull in the land fighting would follow, during which a counterattack by the army would have considerable chance of success.

Toyoda's order called for the Second Fleet to beach itself in front of the Americans on Okinawa and to fire every gun of every ship until the last shell had been expended or the last ship destroyed. None of the ships were expected to return, and individual survivors were told that they could join in the land fighting and 'find glory.'

The order was received aboard Ito's flagship, the *Yamato*, during the afternoon of 5th April, as the operation was scheduled for 8th April. Ito promptly summoned his captains to a conference, and there was a storm of protest. Nearly all the commanding officers objected to the operation – not because it meant certain death, but

because they considered it meant squandering what was left of the Imperial Navy for a very dubious return. There was no question of Ito's subordinates not being prepared to give their lives, and those of their men, for the Emperor. But they were dominated by a philosophy that had come to them long ago through their association with Britain's Royal Navy: 'Fight bravely, but not in vain.' The conference lasted for five hours, during which some heated comments were passed about the planning capabilities of Combined Fleet Headquarters, safe in its air-raid shelter. But discipline held. When Ito said that the order must be obeyed, the argument stopped and the conferees returned to their ships to prepare for the forthcoming action.

On board the ships the return of the captains spelled feverish activity. Bayonets were sharpened ready for the hand-to-hand fighting many of the crews expected to see ashore. Fuel sufficient only for a one way passage

Japanese battleship *Yamato* during the Second Fleet's suicidal attempt to prevent the Okinawa landings

was taken on, and the crews were weeded out, only those needed to man the ships remaining. (Among those who were disembarked was a batch of midshipmen, fresh from the Naval Academy, who had arrived only a few days earlier. Many of these young men wished to take part in the operation but they were not permitted to do so.) Finally there were the farewell parties, at which many bottles of *sake* were consumed. These broke up with the singing of 'Doki no Sakura' ('Cherry Blossoms of the same rank') – an old Naval Academy song.

The Second Fleet steamed out of the Inland Sea that night, and by 6am on 6th April it was southwest of Kyushu, heading due south for Okinawa on a zig-zag course. If all went well it was scheduled to reach the American landing beaches just before daylight on the 8th. An anti-sub-

125

Yamato is sunk after an attack by 300 US aircraft off Okinawa

marine formation was assumed after the ships passed through the Bungo Strait, and for some hours twenty Zeros of the Fifth Air Fleet provided an aerial umbrella. But as land receded the Zeros returned, and the reconnaissance seaplanes from the *Yamato* and *Yahagi* were flown off to prevent their destruction in the forthcoming battle. There was no need for reconnaissance; the whereabouts of the Americans was well known – just as the Americans knew of their approach. Five miles behind Ito's fleet the US submarines *Threadfin* and *Hackleback* trailed the fleet and watched in fascination as the monstrous *Yamato* moved across their periscopes. At dawn on 7th April US flying boats arrived to tighten the watch.

Low, heavy clouds provided perfect protection for the attackers when the Americans struck at 12.30pm. Shortly

after noon the *Yamato*'s radar had picked up two large formations of planes converging on her, and the first of them appeared overhead even before the message had been relayed to the other ships. There was no question of changing course, but the fleet speeded up to twenty-seven knots, swung into two lines with 5,000 yard intervals between ships, and opened fire. From start to finish Ito's fleet stood little chance. Although the *Yamato*'s AA guns put up a formidable curtain of steel, it was of little use. Planes were shot down but new attack waves came on incessantly. This was the fourth time the Americans had attacked the giant battleship and they were determined to sink her on this occasion.

The first bomb struck the *Yamato* at 12.40pm, and ten minutes later a torpedo found its mark. Thereafter many more bombs and at least fifteen torpedoes struck home. Three hours of steady attack finally doomed the great battleship. In all 300 US carrier-based planes hit Ito's ship. By 15.00, not only *Yamato*, but the *Yahagi* and two destroyers *Asashimo* and *Kamakaze* had all been sunk. Two other destroyers the *Isokaze* and *Kasumi*, dead in the water, were sunk by other Japanese destroyers, after their crews had been rescued. Of the fleet only five destroyers now remained, and they returned to port next day. This greatest of suicide actions which was aborted had cost Japan six out of ten ships and the lives of more than 2,500 men.

After the battle Combined Fleet Headquarters issued a communiqué which read: 'Owing to the brave and sacrificial fighting of the Second Fleet, our Special Attack planes achieved great result.' The truth was that this last desperate fleet sortie of the Imperial Navy had ended in a miserable failure. The once glorious Combined Fleet, which had prided itself on commanding the waters of the entire Western Pacific, had been driven ignominiously from the seas surrounding Japan.

The major phase of *Kikusui* Operation No 1 had achieved nothing, But the subsidiary operations which continued throughout April, May and June scored some minor successes. Ohnishi's planes came down from Kyushu and 1,465 kamikaze planes took part in day and night attacks on targets at Okinawa. These attacks accounted for the heaviest of all kamikaze-inflicted damage. According to the official report of the Commander-in-Chief US Pacific Fleet twenty-six American ships were sunk, and 164 damaged by suicide attacks between 6th April and 22nd June. This figure included the victims of sporadic, small-scale suicide efforts which occupied another 200 Japanese Army and Navy planes.

During April the *Okhas* scored their first hit. After the *Okha* sortie of 21st March had ended so ignominiously, there was some hesitation about selecting the right moment and proper conditions for using this weapon again. But the opportunity presented itself on 12th April when *Okha* sorties were ordered as part of *Kikusui* Operation No 2. Eight *Okhas* participated in this day's attack, along with eighty kamikaze planes and more than one hundred escort fighters. They headed for Okinawa by varying courses to converge on the island from different directions. The bombers carrying them also flew low, in order to take advantage of the high cliffs which surrounded the American anchorages off the island.

Of the eight mother planes in this attack, six were shot down after making their release and only one returned to base to relate the dramatic story of how the pilot of one *Okha*, Lieutenant Saburo Dolii, had performed his mission. Dolii, twenty-two years old, appears to have been a placid and somewhat taciturn individual. During the flight out of Okinawa he slept on a pile of sacks in the back of the Betty bomber. Wakened as they approached the target area, he shook hands with the crew before climbing through the bomb bay into his tiny rocket-powered craft. A battleship was selected as his objective and he was released 20,000 yards from his target at an altitude of about 7,000 feet. Last seen by the crew of the bomber as it turned west for safety, Dolii was plummeting down towards the American ships surrounding his battleship. Later, they said, a column of black smoke could be seen belching from the general location of the target. Whether Dolii hit a US ship, or whether the damage should be attributed to one of the other *Okha* pilots will never be known. But that day the destroyer *Mannert L Abele* was sunk and the destroyer *Stanley* damaged by piloted 'Baka bombs', as the Americans called the *Okhas*.

This operation proved the worth of the *Okha* to the Japanese and after this the piloted bombs were used regularly. All in all a total of seventy-four *Okha* missions were despatched before the war came to an end. Of

Left: A kamikaze plane over *USS Vicksburg* starts its crash-dive. *Above:* The blazing flight deck of the US carrier *Bunker Hill. Below:* A direct suicide hit on *New Mexico* during the Japanese *Kikusui* operation

these fifty-six were either released from their carrier planes, or shot down while still attached to them. While many *Okha* dives were reported as successful, confirmation was questionable. After the war the Americans estimated that only four ever hit a target, and claimed that the weapon was a fiasco. 'It failed', wrote Admiral J J Clark, 'because it was a one shot mission – the pilots never got any practice!' Yet, even if the *Okha* failed to do much material damage, there can be little doubt that the appearance of piloted suicide bombs had a telling effect on the morale of the American sailors.

The *Okha* bomb attacks were, of course, supplementary to what might be termed the more 'conventional' kamikaze strikes. These went on continuously, and although the suicide pilots failed to sink any capital ships during the eighty-two days and nights of their assaults they did come close to eliminating the giant carrier *Enterprise*. Variously called 'The Big E', 'The Lucky E', 'The Old Lady', and 'The Galloping Ghost of the Oahu Coast', the *Enterprise* had seen action in every major American sea battle since the beginning of the war. She had destroyed more than seventy enemy warships and had shot down nearly 1,000 planes. Six times the ghost carrier had been reported sunk.

On 14th May 1945 planes from the *Enterprise* took off on a mission to strike at airfields in southern Japan. Next morning twenty-five kamikazes roared in from the southwest and headed for the carrier. One after another they were shot down or missed the target and crashed into the sea. Nevertheless one Zero kamikaze got through, to smash his plane into the very centre of the carrier. After crashing through three decks and killing fourteen American seamen, the Zero's bomb exploded and only quick work by the ship's damage-control crew saved the *Enterprise*.

The *kaiten* operations were no more successful than the flamboyant lem-ming-like self-destruction of the Second Fleet. After the ill-conceived Tatara operation the *I-58* was ordered to support the Second Fleet action with *kaiten* attacks on the US ships lured out by the *Yamato*. Spotted by American aircraft she never got near any of the US capital ships. Harried and chased day and night by destroyers and aircraft its captain eventually called off the operations and returned to port with his *kaiten* intact.

I-58 was lucky to get back to Japan. Eight other Japanese submarines were sunk during April and, with the Sixth Fleet's *kaiten* carriers reduced to four, a heated argument developed on how the 'Heaven-shakers' should be employed in future operations. The Naval General Staff in Tokyo, and Combined Fleet Headquarters, still believed that the best way was against American fleets and fleet bases. But Commander Tennosuke Torisu, the torpedo expert on the staff of the Sixth Fleet Headquarters argued fiercely against this. He claimed that

kaiten should be sent well out to sea to disrupt the Americans' lines of communications. Eventually Tokyo agreed to let two submarines make attacks on supply lines. Their performance would be evaluated and a final decision would be taken on how the *kaiten* would operate in the future.

I-47 and *I-36* were selected for the experiment, and they sallied forth on 20th and 23rd April respectively. Each was carrying six *kaiten*. *I-47* headed for an area through which US ships bound for Okinawa from Ulithi would have to pass, while *I-36* made for a similar interception zone between Okinawa and Saipan. *I-36* drew the first blood. Soon after dawn on 27th April she ran into a convoy of thirty ships bound for Okinawa. At 8,000 yards distance orders were given for all six *kaiten* to be fired. Four got away, but two were jammed in their racks. Ten minutes later four successive explosions shook the submarine. That night a report was radioed to Tokyo claiming 'four victims, 'estimated to be transports or cargo ships'.

Coming when it did, this success seemed an appropriate sacrificial offering to the Emperor, whose birthday was on 29th April. In fact only one vessel was sunk, the *SS Canada Victory*, so it must be assumed that all four *kaiten* pilots, Lieutenant Yagi and Petty Officers Abe, Matsuka and Ebihara, had aimed for the same ship.

During the night of 1st May, *I-47*'s captain, the redoubtable Orita, also encountered a convoy. Because the *kaiten* were virtually blind in the dark, he decided to attack with conventional torpedoes. Twelve hours later, however, an opportunity came to use the suicide weapons and two *kaiten* (Lieutenant Kakizake and Petty Officer Yamaguchi) were fired at targets reported to be a transport escorted by a destroyer. When two explosions were heard in quick succession it was assumed that both targets had been hit. But when Orita raised his periscope he could see a

USS Enterprise, The Big E, is hit by a kamikaze aircraft

The American forces on Okinawa throw in everything to try to dislodge the Japanese defenders

destroyer about three miles away. Another *kaiten* was launched, and a long delayed explosion eventually suggested that Petty Officer Furukawa had gone to Yasukuni. Four days later two of the three remaining *kaiten*, Lieutenant Maeda and Petty Officer Shinkai, were fired at a 'cruiser'. Orita's intention had been to fire all three, but when the telephone link to the last *kaiten* broke down, Petty Officer Yokota lived to tell the tale. 'To live, at times, is much more difficult than to die . . . A lot of patience is required to wait until the best possible moment for dying comes.' These words were used by Orita as consolation when Yokota protested at being deprived of the opportunity to give his life.

I-47 now followed *I-36* back to Japan. After their return a conference in Tokyo concluded that the success of the two most recent sorties justified Commander Torisu's views. Submarine operations would now be left entirely in the hands of the Sixth Fleet Headquarters. Admiral Nagai promptly ordered every available *I*-class submarine, a total of nine, to be despatched on *kaiten* operations in the western Pacific. By mid-July six had been sunk, but the Japanese claimed that the *kaitens* sank 15 tankers and transports, 2 cruisers, 5 destroyers, 1 seaplane tender and 6 unidentified ships in the last three months of the war. These figures were subsequently declared by the Allies to be spurious. Eighty *kaiten* pilots were killed in action, and even if they had sent down eighty ships it is doubtful whether they could have changed the outcome of the land battle for Okinawa.

When the Americans first stormed ashore on Okinawa they had expected an immediate and vicious response from the garrison. To everybody's surprise the defenders offered little resistance, and the landing beaches were secured in the face of only a mild defence. Not until the US troops started to move inland was the pattern of previous assaults repeated. Then the Americans experienced another version of the storming of Iwo Jima. The defenders fought desperately, inflicting heavy casualties on the invaders. But gradually they were pushed back to the hills in the southern part of the island. By V-E Day, 8th May, the Japanese were beaten.

In the next three weeks General Ushijima managed to perform a minor miracle by organising another line of defence. But he knew the end was close. And by this time the Japanese troops knew it also. Bombarded by millions of leaflets which assured them of fair treatment a few considered the idea of laying down their arms. But most decided against it and committed suicide instead.

Admiral Ota's naval force made a final Banzai charge on 13th June against the forces which had landed in the vicinity of Oroku. Nothing more is known of Ota and his men. The last message received from him was sent on 6th June:

'More than two months have passed since we engaged the invaders. In complete unity and harmony with the Army, we have made every effort to crush the enemy . . .

'. . . I tender herewith my deepest apology to the Emperor for my failure to better defend the Empire, the grave task with which I was entrusted.

'The troops under my command have fought gallantly, in the finest tradition of the Japanese Navy. Fierce bombing and bombardments may deform the mountains of Okinawa but cannot alter the loyal spirit of our men. We hope and pray for the perpetuation of the Empire and gladly give our lives for that goal.

'To the Navy Minister and all my superior officers I tender my sincerest appreciation and gratitude for their kindness of many years. At the same time, I earnestly beg you to give thoughtful consideration to the families of my men who fall at this outpost as soldiers of the Emperor.

Above: The crew of a suicide bomber which crash-landed on Okinawa
Below: The suicide monument to the Japanese banzai on Okinawa

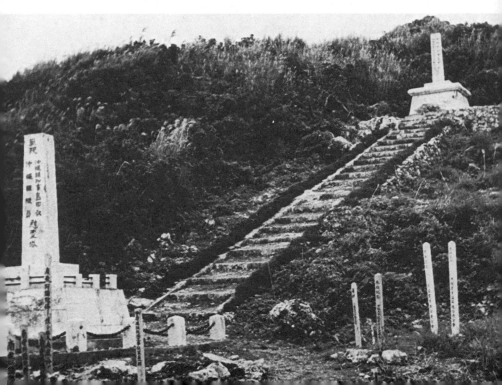

US bombers attack a Japanese warship
at anchor off the coast of Japan

'With my officers and men I give three cheers for the Emperor and pray for the everlasting peace of the Empire.

Though my body decay in remote Okinawa,

My spirit will persist in defence of the homeland.

Minoru Ota
Naval Commander'.

Before he perished Ota is known to have issued one order which typifies the suicidal attitude of his kind. A huge cave inside the Japanese lines was serving as a field hospital and 300 badly wounded Japanese Marines of Ota's detachment lay there. Fearing that the Americans would flush out the cave with flamethrowers before asking questions, Ota ordered the senior medical officer to make sure the patients had an honourable death without any further suffering. The doctor and his orderlies walked along the long rows of sick men and methodically squeezed hypodermic syringes into 300 outstretched arms.

Above: Over 100,000 Japanese on Okinawa chose to die rather than surrender. *Right:* Generals Ushijima and Cho both commit 'hara kiri'

No-one appears to quite know what happened to Tanamachi's 7,000 airmen. Like many of the army units they probably fought on until they were annihilated. That at least was what happened to one isolated detachment whose commanding officer reported in a final message: 'My men are in high spirits and fighting gallantly. We pray for the final victory of the motherland. We will fight to the last man in defence of this outpost . . .'

Inside the cave which sheltered his headquarters General Ushijima relaxed with a bottle of whiskey while he listened to the reports coming from his scattered units. His last defence line had disintegrated and the Japanese troops had become a disorganised rabble, skulking in holes, hungry and without hope. Ushijima was a realist and he knew that it was finished.

Quietly he dictated a farewell message to Tokyo:

'To my great regret we are no longer able to continue the fight. For this failure I tender deepest apologies to the Emperor and the people of the homeland. We will make one final charge to kill as many of the enemy as possible. I pray for the souls of men killed in battle and for the prosperity of the Imperial Family.

'Death will not quell the desire of my spirit to defend the homeland.

'With deepest appreciation of the kindness and co-operation of my superiors and my colleagues in arms, I bid farewell to all of you forever.'

A poetic postscript to his letter read:

'Green grass dies in the islands without waiting for fall,

But it will be reborn verdant in the springtime of the homeland.

Weapons exhausted, our blood will bathe the earth, but the spirit will survive;

Our spirits will return to protect the motherland.'

Only the final ceremonious exit remained now. And in the early morning of 22nd June, Ushijima and his chief of staff, General Isama Cho, dressed themselves in their best uniforms and pinned their medals to their tunics. A quilt had been laid out on a narrow ledge of rock just outside the cave. Over it was a white sheet symbolising death. The two generals knelt. According to the Samurai code *hara-kiri* is supposed to be committed facing towards the Imperial Palace in Tokyo. Because of the narrowness of the ledge Ushijima and Cho had to face west to the Pacific. A staff officer handed the two generals each a knife. Then came *seppuku* – the slash across the abdomen. Behind Ushijima another officer raised his sword and quickly struck off Ushijima's head. Cho was decapitated in the same way a few moments later.

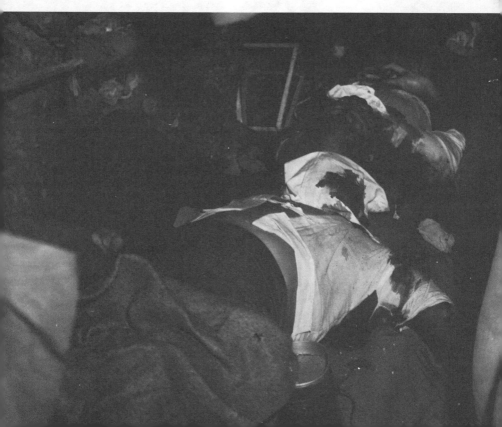

The battle for Okinawa was over. But not the dying, since Ushijima's example was followed by the most grotesque series of suicides. Naked Japanese soldiers would dash out of their caves, hurl rocks at the Americans and then race back behind the rocks to slit their throats or blow themselves up with grenades. A particularly bizarre incident occurred when a patrol of US Marines suddenly found themselves in a clearing surrounded by a strong force of Japanese accompanied by a number of women. With unusual presence of mind, the patrol commander smiled, pulled out his cigarettes and offered them around. A few of the Japanese soldiers dropped their weapons and reached for the cigarettes. Their officers not only refused but turned away. Then one drove his sword straight through his woman companion, handed his sword and wristwatch to one of the Americans, stepped back and blew off his head with a grenade. This infected the others who promptly killed the other women and then committed suicide. For two hours the US patrol was compelled to watch a suicidal blood-bath.

In the fighting for Okinawa Japanese casualties amounted to more than a 100,000 killed. Of these deaths at least half were incurred in suicidal operations. Strategically the Americans had won a great victory, for they were now on Japan's very doorstep. But their butcher's bill was also high – more than 12,500 killed and missing, twice the casualty rate of Iwo Jima.

Okinawa was now to become the final base for the invasion of the Japanese home islands. November 1945 was the date contemplated, and bloody battle was forecast. In it a large proportion of the Japanese nation was expected to seek self-immolation.

Cataclysmic finale

During July the kamikaze and *kaiten* attacks continued on targets round Okinawa. Still the Americans were undeterred. By the middle of the month US ships were standing off Japan's shoreline, shelling Japanese cities with their big guns. Waves of carrier based planes filled the skies and repeatedly attacked Tokyo and the big naval bases at Kure and Yokosuka. The last of Japan's warships were anchored at Kure, waiting to sortie and strike the American invaders in one last desperate gesture. While they waited the American planes sank the aircraft carriers *Amagi* and *Kaiyo*, the battleships *Haruna*, *Ise*, and *Hyuga*, three carriers and a destroyer. Japan had only a single battleship left now, the *Nagato*. Badly damaged she was the only Japanese battleship to survive the war.

Yet Japan was prepared to fight on. In the homeland there were more than 100,000 troops with plenty of guns and ammunition. Dozens of *kaiten* had been secreted along the coasts of Kyushi, Shikoku and Honshu. There were still 10,000 planes available. And the greatest asset of all: there were still plenty of men willing and anxious to die for their Emperor.

Plans were drawn up in Tokyo for Operation Decision. This was to be a final all-out assault on the American invasion forces massing at Okinawa. Many of the aircraft were obsolete and some were only slow old trainers, but they could all be used in kamikaze attacks. A hundred new five-man submarines, called *koryu*, and 300 new two-man submarines, called *kairyu*, were also beginning to roll off the production lines. Both *koryu* and *kairyu* had been designed to carry two torpedoes apiece. At the last minute the *kairyu* were modified. Instead of torpedoes, special warheads were fitted in the bow, which contained 1,000 pounds of explosive. Like the *kaiten* the

Now that the Allies were poised to invade Japan, would the Japanese turn the invasion into a blood-bath?

kairyu would be used as suicide weapons. There was also the *shinyo*. These were small light and fast motorboats about fifteen feet long. They were intended to crash into enemy ships at night, at a speed of more than twenty knots. Some *shinyo* were sent to Okinawa but more than 2,000 of them were scattered in coves and inlets along Japan's lengthy coastline. Some were hidden inside Japan's harbours, where they could attack the Allies when they thought they were safe, achored in a conquered port. There too, the *Fukuyuru*, strong swimmers with mines attached to their backs, would launch their suicidal attacks.

The Japanese high command had appreciated, correctly in fact, that the Americans would try to establish their first bridgehead in Japan on the southern island of Kyushu and would follow it with a second landing in the peninsula east of Tokyo. Troops were deployed in anticipation, with 3,000

Above and right : **Japanese *koryu* submarines, each carrying a crew of five, fitted with two torpedoes**

kamikaze planes to support operations on the southern island and 1,000 on the northern one. Some Japanese politicians were now talking about the need to end the war before Japan was completely destroyed. But the military were prepared to fight to the bitter end. To inflict thousands of Allied casualties they were prepared to throw away hundreds of thousands of Japanese lives. Many people in Japan were prepared to accept the sacrifice. In rural areas farmers had armed themselves with bamboo spears to tackle the expected paratroopers. *Samurai* slogans were posted in public places; radio broadcasts and newspapers made emotional appeals to the patriotic fervour of the Japanese citizen. 1,000,000 men had died in the home islands of Japan; 5,000,000 houses had been destroyed and 9,000,000 more

One of many last-ditch weapons developed by Japan in her last effort to stave off defeat was the Shinyo suicide boat. They were armed with a large charge of HE or two depth charges in the bows, the idea being that the pilot would set a collision course with a worthwhile Allied target, arm the explosive and then hold on till he collided with the ship. It was hoped that these craft would cause enough damage to sink a medium sized vessel. By the end of the war about 6,000 Shinyo boats had been built for use at Okinawa and in Japan, but so far as is known, no Allied vessel suffered major damage as a result of one of these craft. They weighed between $1\frac{1}{4}$ and 2 tons, measured $16\frac{1}{2}$ to 18 feet in length and were capable of between 25 and 30 knots on the power of one or two automobile engines. Each craft was equipped with two 5-inch rockets at the stern. The rockets were meant to explode and send out a shower of incendiary bullets to put off the aim of gunners on exposed mounts for guns of 40mm calibre or smaller

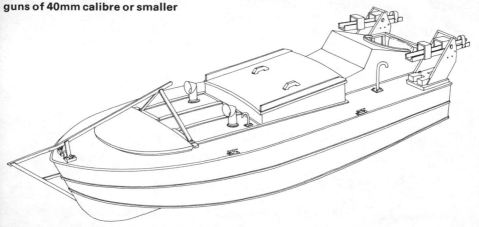

US B-29s demolish 95 per cent of the
Japanese city of Toyama, during their
raid on 1st August 1945

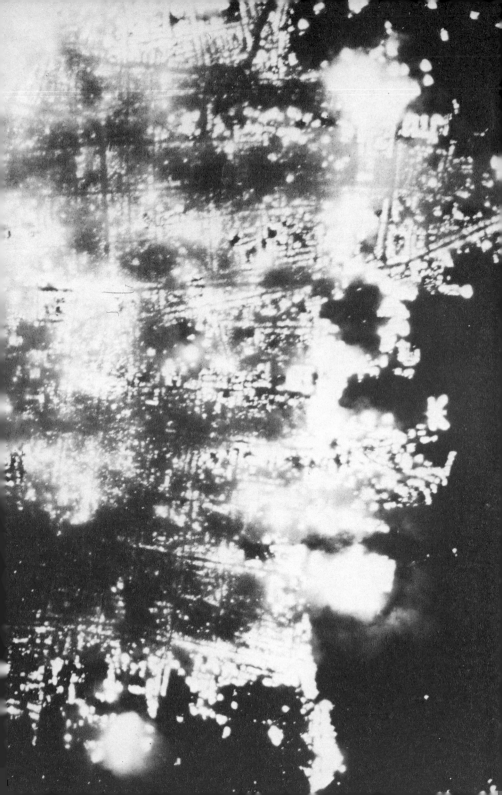

people were homeless; the Imperial Navy had been destroyed; the Army was in dire straits; the only tactic left open to the Japanese Air Force was to rely on kamikazes. Everyone knew the war was going against Japan. Yet millions of Japanese were prepared to give their lives in a desperate attempt to turn the tide.

At the beginning of August the Japanese government made a nationwide announcement that the war had been terminated. This had little effect because the military were still dictating national policies for Japan, even though General Hideki Tojo was out of power and in disgrace. General Anami, the War Minister, issued a statement of his own at the same time as the government announcement. And the Japanese people had become accustomed to heeding the War Minister's words. They must prepare for a terrible fight on Japanese soil, Anami urged. He cited the example of Iyeyasu Tokugawa, the mighty *shogun* who was once besieged in his castle by a vastly superior enemy force. Almost out of food and water, Tokugawa ordered the main gate of the castle to be thrown open. Standing at the entrance he invited his enemies to enter. But they suspected a trap, and withdrew; later Tokugawa conquered them. This, contended Anami, was an ideal analogy. If Japan appeared to let the Americans come on, they too would be defeated. 'We must fight on', he said, '. . . even if we are forced to eat weeds, gnaw sand, and sleep in the hills . . .'

It needed a miracle to stop the projected national blood-bath. And on the 'day of the double dawn', 6th August 1945, the miracle happened when a cataclysmic explosion rocked Hiroshima. Three days later a second atomic bomb destroyed Nagasaki. It was the horrendous loss of lives

Above and right: A total of more than 4,000 aircraft were available for kamikaze use in the defence of the Japanese islands

Above: American B-29s over the Japanese naval arsenal at Kure. *Below:* A portion of devastated Tokyo after an incendiary attack. *Right:* Further incendiary attacks reduce Osaka to rubble

Signals for the end of the war; the atomic blasts at Hiroshima, *above*, and Nagasaki, *right*, prevent a national blood-bath

resulting from these explosions which eventually got past Japan's fanatical death-defying spirit. 75,000 people died at Hiroshima, 40,000 at Nagasaki. But if the war had been fought out, the toll of death and destruction might have been five or six times as great.

The annals of war yield many instances of death-defying tactics. Throughout history soldiers of many nations have been taught that duty must be performed at the risk of life. But in western eyes the deliberate exploitation of Japanese willingness to die for emperor and homeland was the nadir of degraded brutality.

Suicidal attacks with military objectives must, of course, be distinguished from the other forms of self-immolation referred to in this story. Individual *hara-kiri* was an age-old Japanese ritual undertaken as a voluntary act after loss of face. It was a means of regaining honour, and a silent revenge on those in the governmental hierarchy who were so high that they could not be attacked without the aggressor losing respect. *Hara-kiri* was seen as a tragic fate to be accepted, part of the honourable way of life in which the guilt and responsibility of the individual were expiated in a traditional ritual. A comparable code of honour used to exist among German and Austrian officers. If they behaved dishonourably, a loaded pistol was presented to them as a suggestion and command: kill yourself.

Most of the suicides on Saipan and Okinawa had none of the motives which prompted *hara-kiri*, These were instances of a mass reaction which is seen among animals. In the face of danger, ants will sometimes surrender passively to their fate and die. The same can happen to human beings, and such reactions are prevalent in panic situations. When people fail as a group and believe they have no future, they surrender 'en masse' to death. Plutarch describes the self-slaughter

which followed the Roman victory at Vercella. Xenophon relates a comparable experience which followed the storming of a small fortified settlement. Loss of freedom and anticipation of torture can lead to catastrophic reactions – murderous rebellion or self-chosen death. On Okinawa both reactions were observed.

The sucidal attacks of the kamikaze and *kaiten* pilots were in a different category. What distinguished them from all historical precedent was not the absence of any chance of survival but their systematic continuance. These attacks went on from October 1944 until August 1945, and there is no parallel in history. In other wars desperate situations have sometimes called for

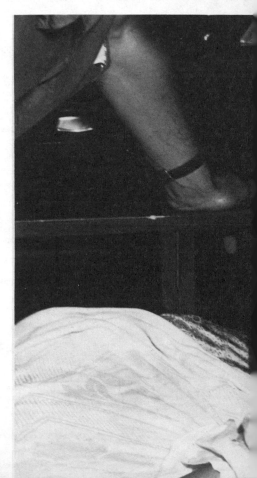

Tojo attempts 'hara-kiri'

desperate remedies. A crisis was followed by a sudden, quick response, and there was little time for the individuals concerned to dwell on their prospects. Moreover, Westerners usually tried to leave some hope of survival. The Japanese military hierarchy resolutely closed the last avenue of escape. Soldiers, sailors and airmen were told that their honourable suicide would turn the tide of war, and their patriotic deed would bring them immortality. To the western mind the acceptance of this idea, and the Japanese serviceman's hypnotic fascination with death is beyond credence.

Today the popular belief is that the Japanese who took part in *banzai* charges, flew kamikaze missions, piloted *kaitens* and *shinyo* 'bang boats', or served as human mines, were all fanatics. Because many of the *banzai* charges were ordered on the spur·of the moment no doubt there was an element of fanatism in the army's operations. But the kamikazes, *kaiten* and *kairyu* men were dedicated individuals whose calm acceptance of death illustrates the impact of ideological persuasion. Fanatical or not, their actions can only be understood when seen in relation to deep-rooted Japanese traditions and a tyrannical governmental structure. The end of the war brought Japan a new form of government. But the traditions linger, and if Japan's existence were threatened in the 'seventies, she would probably have no more difficulty mustering the men to man suicide weapons than she did in 1944 and 1945.

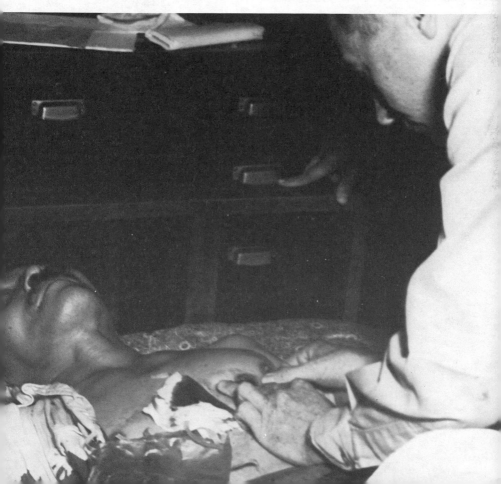

The balance sheet

There is a number of reasons why an accurate quantitative appraisal of the Japanese suicide weapon is not feasible. Apart from the lack of data it is almost impossible to express a morale effect in quantitative terms. The *Banzai* charge was necessarily wasteful. But it was usually an attempt to break out of a hopeless situation, when the only alternative was defeat. On the other hand, the airborne versions of the Banzai charge were also the product of defeat. Yet while the charge was scorned, the *kamikazes* drew the respect of Japan's enemies – possibly because they scored such telling blows. The *kaiten* effort was respected for similar reasons despite the disproportionate dividends it yielded.

SUMMARY OF KAMIKAZE OPERATIONS.
Japanese naval planes expended 1,228
Okha Bombs expended 298
Total sorties flown (includes escorts) 2,314
Total allied vessels *claimed* sunk 81
                 actually sunk 34
                 claimed damaged 195
                 actually damaged 288
Of the Okha bombs only four hit their targets, although the Japanese claimed a much higher figure. However the losses recorded above included 3 escort aircraft carriers, 13 destroyers sunk as well as 8 fleet carriers, 10 battleships and numerous other warships damaged. (*USS St Lo*, *Ommaney Bay* and *Bismarck Sea*.)

SUMMARY OF *KAITEN* OPERATIONS
The Japanese claimed to have sunk forty Allied ships including a British cruiser of the Leander class, with *kaiten*. Eight *I* class submarines and nearly 900 sailors perished in the course of this effort.

   Actual losses inflicted appear to have been limited to the US oiler *Mississinewa*, the destroyer escort *USS Underhill*, and one merchant ship the *SS Canada Victory*.

Bibliography

Kogun: The Japanese Army in the Pacific War by S Hayashi and A D Coox (US Marine Corps, Quantico, Virginia)
Sink Em All by C A Lockwood (Dutton, New York)
Challenge for the Pacific by Robert Leckie (Doubleday, New York. Hodder & Stoughton, London)
Divine Wind by R Inoguchi, T Nakajima and R Pineau (Ballantine Books, New York)
A Ship to Remeber: The Saga of the Hornet by Alexander Griflin (Howell, New York)
Under the Southern Cross: The Saga of the American Division by Francis Cronin (Combat Forces Press, Washington DC)
The Island: A Personal Account of Guadalcanal by Herbert Merillat (Houghton & Mifflin, Boston)
Japan: Past and Present by Edwin Reischauer (Knopf, New York)
The Big E: The Story of the USS Enterprise by Edward Stafford (Random House, New York)
The Night of the New Moon by Laurens van der Post (Hogarth, London)